CW00531372

INDIA

A Sadhu in Amber, Rajasthan. In Hinduism, "sadhu" (Sanskrit: "good man"), is a term of respect for a religious man who leads a life of strict asceticism, as a hermit or a roaming monk relying upon alms.

In some parts of India, a custom typicallly reserved for women is the painting of her hands and feet with henna. This woman's hands in Srinagar are decorated with very elaborate patterns.

ABOUT THIS BOOK

"I honor the place in you in which the entire Universe dwells, I honor the place in you which is of Light, of Love, of Truth, of Peace and of Wisdom. I honor the place in you where when you are in that place, and I am in that place, we are One." This is the answer Mahatma Gandhi is said to have given Albert Einstein when he asked about the meaning of "Namaste", a greeting that in India is more of a gesture than just a word.

Namaste! Welcome to India, a land of powerful sensations, of contrasts and superlatives. No other country has a comparable variety of cultures and religions. After China, it is the most populous country on earth, with traditions developed over five thousand years of history. It stretches from the Himalayas, the tallest mountain range in the world, to Cape Comorin in the subtropical south. The roots of Hinduism, to which about 80 percent of Indians adhere, are found in the prehistoric Indus Valley civilization, and India is the cradle of Buddhism, which forms the foundation of several Asian cultures, from Thailand and Indonesia to Tibet and Cambodia.

In the largest democracy in the world, Christians, Jains, Muslims, Parsis and Sikhs have been able to maintain their identities alongside Hindus and Buddhists. In the land of yogis, sadhus and gurus, spirituality and economic development are not irreconcilable. Thus, despite all the disparities between rich and poor, and between life in the countryside and in the teeming cities, the land and its people still largely maintain a warmth and sincerity that visitors should respond to with a heartfelt "Namaste". In India, a simple gesture will do: Bring the palms of your hands together in front of your heart before making a slight bow.

The breathtaking variety of India and the incredible abundance of attractions — many of which are UNESCO World Heritage Sites — is portrayed in the photographs and short texts of this book and arranged according to geography. The map section makes it easy to find locations and sights, with smart pictograms to help you on your explorations. At the end of the book, the index links the photo and map sections, and provides you with Internet addresses for some of the most important attractions. We hope all of this will help you discover India in all its beauty.

Wolfgang Kunth

The Taj Mahal is one of the most beautiful works of Islamic architecture in the world. It is a mausoleum built by the Great Mogul Shah Jehan in Agra in 1631, in memory of his most beloved wife.

"We pray to Allah, Jesus Christ and Shiva. We have eighteen official languages and more than 500 dialects. One of our tiny minorities is among the richest in the world while most of our people barely have enough food to eat. Some live in snowcapped mountains while the others live in the desert or under shady palm trees. Sharp contrasts, yes, but when the enemy is at our door we stick together through thick and thin! We are one folk!"
Khushwant Singh

CONTENTS

Inset: Wall paintings in the Thikse monastery. Hidden amid Himalayan giants (below), monastic culture in Ladakh has preserved five Tibetan orders: Nyingmapa, Matho, Sakyapa, Drugpa and Drigungpa.

A view of the Bhagirati Range in Uttaranchal, in the Indian portion of the Himalayas. Several advanced climbing routes lead to the top of 6,454-m (21,176-ft) Bhagirati III (far right).

THE HIMALAYAS

The world's tallest mountain range, the Himalayas, stretches over 2,400 km (1,500 miles) and separates the Indian subcontinent from the Tibetan plateau. Of the fourteen peaks over 8,000 m (26,000 ft) high, only one is in Indian territory, the Kangchenjunga. Religious Buddhists and Hindus bow in awe before this silent symbol of unapproachable divinity. The mountain is roughly sixty million years old, comprises several chains and is actually still growing, albeit at a rate of only about an inch per year.

Prized for its plush white-gray winter coat, the snow leopard has been hunted to near extinction. Along with many endangered animal species, this region is also home to numerous indigenous flowers like these geraniums, poppies and rhododendrons (right).

Nanda Devi and the "Valley of Flowers" National Parks

The region around the 7,816-m-high (25,643-ft) Nanda Devi peak, which straddles the borders of Nepal and China, is an important refuge for endangered plant and animal species and is also a UNESCO World Heritage Site. Created in 1980, the Nandi Devi National Park is home to snow leopards, musk deer, large herds of bharal (wild sheep) and goral (an antelope-like ungulate). Adjacent to Nanda Devi is the "Valley of Flowers" National Park, famous for its splendid meadows and native plant species, among which are the Himalayan maple (acer caesium), the Indian poppy (meconopsis aculeata) and a variety of snow lotus (saussurea atkinsonii). The valley, which lies not very far from the inhospitable High Himalayas and plays a prominent role in Hindu mythology, is also home to some rare animals such as the Asiatic black bear. "Nanda Devi" means "Goddess of Peace".

Small rowboats take you between the lakeshore and the houseboats. The oars are fashioned into heart shapes. Some houseboat owners have built luxury versions of their homes to accommodate guests.

Dal Lake

Scenic Dal Lake is nestled into the gorgeous foothills of the Himalayas at an elevation of 1,800 m (5,900 ft) above sea level, in a high valley in controversial region of Kashmir. "Shikaras", the gondola-like boats used for transport on the lake – glide silently across the shallow waters as blossoming fields of pink lotus and tall reeds line the shores, forming borders between the floating gardens. Idyllic houseboats made of fragrant cedarwood are anchored all around the lake. The comfortable boats have verandas, sitting rooms with cashmere rugs, dining areas, and bedrooms. On summer mornings, the floating market offers cucumbers, ladyfingers (okra), Kashmir apples, walnuts and of course hot local chilies. Quiet settles on the lake during the cold winter, when people wrap themselves in thick woolen coats and cook on small wood-burning stoves.

The Shah Hamadan mosque (right) is one of the most important landmarks in Srinigar. It is located in the Old Town, whose market (far right, top) features not only goods for sale, but also freshly baked naan flatbread (far right, center). Far right, bottom: A houseboat owner.

Srinagar

Located on the shores of magnificent Dal Lake, Srinagar is the summer capital of the Indian state of Jammu and Kashmir. Winds from the Jhelum River blow noiselessly through the rows of buildings, and canals slice through the Old Town. Striking mosques dominate the townscape, such as the 14th-century Shah Hamadan, which is reminiscent of a pagoda. The most beloved mosque is the Friday Mosque, constructed entirely of wood – as most of the buildings are here. On the eastern edge of the city are the Shalimar Bagh and Nishat Bagh gardens, built by Mughal emperors in an attractive symmetrical layout. Numerous springs feed the canals and cascades that flow between flower beds and avenues of shade trees down to Dal Lake. Since the time of Akbar in the 16th century, Mughal rulers built private garden paradises here where they sought relief during the hot summer months.

Muslims pray to Allah in Srinagar's Dastgir Mosque, while Buddhist monks conjure gods and demons in the Karsha monastery in Ladakh (below and inset). Precious wool is spun from the undercoat of the Cashmere goat (right). Far right: Chili peppers being dried and collected.

KASHMIR — LAND OF CONTRASTS

The former Princely State of Kashmir lies in a majestic mountain region of the north-western Himalayas and Karakoram Range. Because of its optimal location, however, it is a divided country. The state of Jammu and Kashmir is administered by India while the Northern Areas and Azad Kashmir are administered by neighboring Pakistan.

China also partly occupies the Ladakh region. Indeed, within the Indian state of Jammu and Kashmir, the geographical and cultural differences could hardly be greater. The lowlands (Jammu) are Hindu dominated; in the Himalayan foothills (Kashmir), muslims are more than ninety percent of the population; and the high

mountain desert of Ladakh is mostly ethnic Tibetans Buddhists. Most of the time, Kashmir refers to the fertile Kashmir Valley, which has a pleasant climate, evergreen coniferous forests and an idyllic network of lakes around Srinigar, the winter capital. The wealth and beauty of the region has made it a bone of contention between

India and Pakistan since 1947. Add to this the obvious religious differences and it is no surprise there were two wars in 1965 and 1971. Since the outbreak of civil unrest in 1989, things have been tense, but diplomatic efforts have succeeded in inspiring hopes of peace once again in what many refer to as Paradise on Earth.

The earliest royal residence in Leh is said to have been in the Namgyal Tsemo temple (below). Zanskar (right) is a remote region in western Ladakh. Far right: Lingshed monastery. Top middle: The turqoise-studded headdresses of Ladakh women are called "peraks".

Ladakh

The mountain passes around here are certainly not for the faint of heart. Unpaved, steep, and serpentine at best, they wind towards Leh, the capital of Ladakh in the western Himalayas that is dominated by the nine-storey Leh Palace (1630s). Glaciers, raging torrents, and windswept plateaus at 3,000 m (10,000 ft) are typical of Ladakh's wild and beautiful scenery, which often resembles a lunar landscape. Heavy snowdrifts make the passes impenetrable during the winter, cutting the Ladakhis off from the outside world for months. The strategically important military roads on the Pakistani-Chinese border actually follow ancient caravan routes from Tibet into Punjab and from Central Asia into India. The high desert is one of the driest regions in Asia – a stark but stunning spot at the edge of the roof of the world, and a stronghold of Tibetan Buddhism.

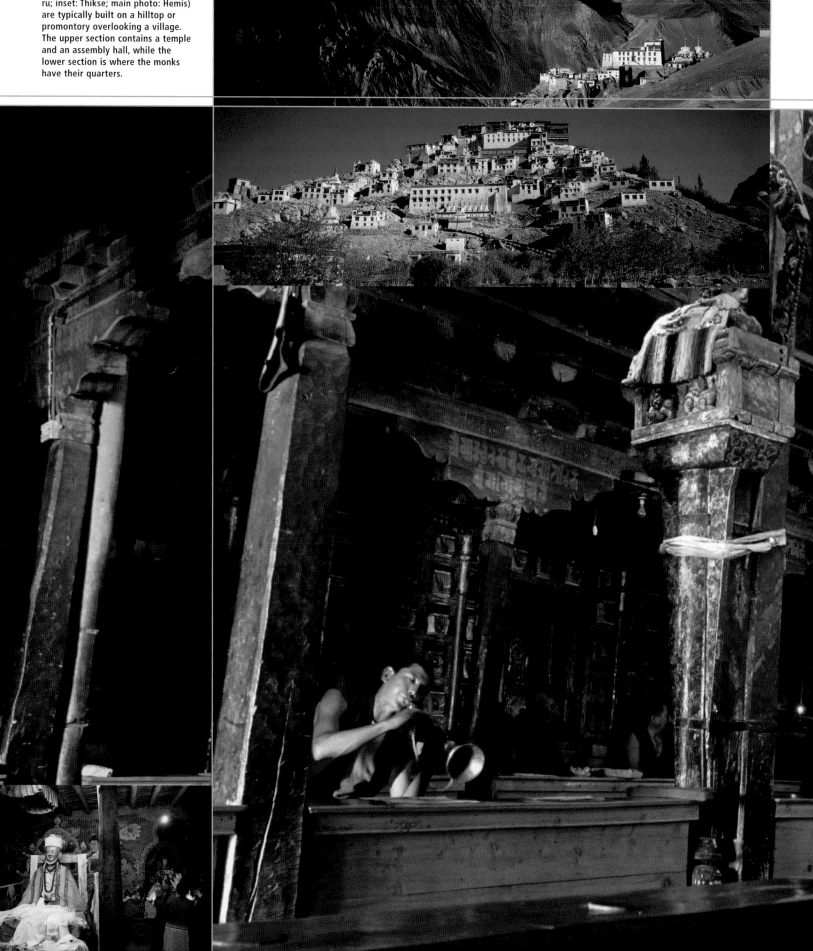

Ladakh's monasteries (right: Lamayuru; inset: Thikse; main photo: Hemis) are typically built on a hilltop or promontory overlooking a village. The upper section contains a temple and an assembly hall, while the lower section is where the monks have their quarters.

Lamayuru, Tikse, Hemis

Afterc clearing the Fatu La pass, at 4,000 m (13,000 ft) the highest of three passes between Srinagar and Leh, you see the Lamayuru gompa, or fortified monastery believed to have been founded in the 11th century. South of Leh, Ladakh's capital located at the junction of ancient caravan routes, is the Thikse gompa, an architectural gem from the 15th century that rises majestically above the Indus Valley. Since the death of reform-minded leader, Tsongkhapa, in 1419, it has been the Ladakh headquarters of the Gelugpa monks. Another breathtaking jewel is the Hemis monastery, south-east of Leh. Founded in the 1630s on orders from King Sengge Namgyal, it belongs to the Drugpa order and is known for its yearly summer festival (June/July), celebrated in honor of Padmasambhava, who spread the Buddhist faith here in the 8th century.

The wall paintings at the Tabo monastery in the Spiti valley (far left) are one of the greatest treasures of Tibetan Buddhist history. In the assembly hall, clay figures represent the chief Buddhist deities (top right). Main photo and top left: Inside the Spituk monastery near Leh.

The most widespread form of Buddhism in the Himalayan region of India is known as Lamaism, or Tibetan Buddhism. It is a monastic religion with its roots in the Bön spiritual tradition of Tibet – a pre-Buddhist, shamanistic, and animistic (souls are attributed to natural entities) system – and in the redemptive teachings of the Buddha.

At its center is the concept that everything in existence is an illusion. Redemption lies in the complete awareness of this truth, which can be obtained in steps, through meditation, yoga, and a complex system of rituals. The Indian monk and missionary Padmasambhava, who in the middle of the eighth century founded the move-

ment's first monastery and ordained the first monks, is considered the founder of Lamaism. His followers were called "red hats" after the color of their headwear. Today, Buddhism The Himalayas comprises many schools and sects. Unreformed red hats (Sakyapa, Kargyupa, Kadampa) follow the teachings of Padmasambhava while

other ancient yogis echo the Bön tradition. As a reaction to increasing secularization, Tsongkhapa, who died in 1419, founded the reform movement of the "yellow hats" and the "School of Virtue", which calls for discipline and strict morals in the monasteries as well as the restriction of occult practices.

Alchi is located on a bend in the Indus valley, the historical and cultural heart of Ladakh (below). With its elaborate woodwork and beatuiful wall paintings (right), the monastery is one of the most important expressions of the Buddhist faith The Himalayas.

Alchi

Hidden in a grove of apricot trees, the 11th-century Alchi monastery is a jewel of early Lamaistic culture and represents the zenith of Himalayan temple architecture. The temple's founder, Rinchen Zangpo, summoned two hundred and thirty builders, woodworkers, stuccoists and painters to build his house of worship. Among the artistic treasures are the door and window lintels carved from poplar wood, the nearly thousand-year-old fluted wooden columns and the 4-m-high (13-ft) plaster statues of the three bodhisattvas (from the Sanskrit: "enlightened beings"): Avalokiteshvara, Maitreya and Manjusri. The elegant lines of the detailed painting on the flowing robes of these holy figures and the fine wall frescoes – above all the circular mandalas, which are used as an aid in meditation – in the main Sumtsek temple are particularly remarkable .

India's Hindu pantheon is rich in its variety, and each god is honored differently. No deity is more popular than Ganesh (main photo and right), the potbellied, elephant-headed god of wisdom and calligraphy. Far right: Shiva, one of Hinduism's main deities. Inset: Goddess, Kali.

THE HINDU PANTHEON

While the historical Buddha, Siddharta Gautama, emphasized that humans are responsible for freeing themselves from the sufferings of life, Hinduism offered its followers a pantheon of deities to reflect the different aspects of the god living within every one of us. Reverence of the forces of nature eventually led to the creation of the sun god Surya, the moon god Chandra, the fire god Agni, and the wind god Vayu. At the apex of the divine order is the many-faceted Shiva, the creator, sustainer and destroyer, who appears in an astonishing variety of incarnations, such as the destructive Bhairava or the cosmic dancer, Nataraja. Vaishnavas, on the other hand, worship Vishnu in ten incarnations (or "avatars") as creator and sustainer. He is especially popular in the form of the shepherd boy Krishna or as Lord Rama, the hero of the epic Ramayana. Shiva's wife, Parvati is known as a merciful goddess (Uma), as a terrifying demon fighter (Durga) and as a bloodthirsty annihilator (Kali). And, of course, no Hindu household is complete without a figure of Ganesh, the elephant-headed son of Shiva and Parvati and god of wisdom, who removes obstacles. Lakshmi, Vishnu's wife and the goddess of luck, and Saraswati, consort of Brahma, creator of the world, and goddess of art and science, complete the list of the main Hindu deities.

Musicians in Kullu (below) celebrate the victory of good over evil with blaring fanfare. Kullu, the "Valley of the Living Gods", is considered the birthplace of Rama in the Hindu epic Ramayana. The Dussehra Festival is celebrated throughout India. Right: A procession in Amritsar.

THE DUSSEHRA HINDU FESTIVAL IN KULLU

On the tenth day of the moonlit half of the Hindu month of Ashvayuja (also known as Ashvina) – in the Gregorian calendar usually early or mid-October – Hindus celebrate the Dasara festival. The festival is known by different names in the different regions of India, and even the fundamental legends, customs and traditions vary considerably. In Kullu, a picturesque valley in the Himalayan foothills, for example, hundreds of masks of deities made of gold and silver are carried into the valley in grand processions. To the accompaniment of blaring shenais (reeded horns), the local residents of this mountainous region lead the way, followed by holy men who fall repeatedly into trances. Homage is paid to Raghunatha, an incarnation of the god Vishnu, who resides in the temple of the raja of Kullu above the town. Being the chief protective deity of the valley, he is brought to the festival square in a wooden temple carriage and installed in his glittering festival tent before a cheering crowd. For an entire week, locals and visitors join in the festivities celebrating another victory of good over evil. Part of the festival includes a market (mela) that features fortune-tellers, medicine men, and holy men offering their skills for alms and donations. For most of the locals this is the high point of the year.

Right: Monks from Sangacholing, Sikkim's oldest monastery (1697), carry prayer flags up to the temple. Below: "Wind horses" – the English translation for the Tibetan term for prayer flags, "rlung rta" – fluttering in the wind in the Dzongri La pass.

Sikkim

Kangchenjunga (8,597 m/28,205 ft), India's only mountain over 8,000 m, is located in the former kingdom of Sikkim. Its summits – the "Five Jewels of Eternal Snow" – are considered sacred and should not be climbed, in order to avoid the ire of the gods. Even nowadays, the regions bordering Nepal, Tibet and Bhutan, which after a plebiscite joined India as its twenty-second state in 1975, can only be entered by special permission. This land of gorges and endless rice terraces enjoys a variety of climatic zones ranging from subtropical to high alpine, and hundreds of wild orchid species display their magnificent blossoms under the shade of the forest canopy. The abundant native flora includes over four thousand plants. The ancient tree fern, going back to the carboniferous period, is a rarity, as are the diverse varieties of over thirty rhododendron.

Inset: New Delhi's main bazaar in the Paharganj District is just a short walk from the New Delhi railway station. Backpackers as well as locals stock up on the most necessary items here.

Below: Agra is on the west bank of the Yamuna river. It owes its importance to the Mughal emperors who built the city's Red Fort. There is a fantastic view from here all the way to the Taj Mahal.

DELHI AND THE NORTH

The plentiful rivers and lush landscape of the north provided the foundation for early Indian civilizations. These alluvial plains are, after all, the birthplace of Hinduism, Buddhism and Jainism. Old Delhi, the city of 17th-century Mughal emperor Shah Jahan, has miraculously maintained its medieval character while New Delhi presents an image of imperial grandeur: After twenty years of construction it was made the capital of British India. It was also here that Indian independence was declared on August 15, 1947.

In the Hindu religion fire ("agni") is the earthly incarnation of the Divine in the form of a flame. This is why fire plays a large role in festive ceremonies, as shown below during a procession in Amritsar. Right: Inside the city's temple complex.

Amritsar

The holy city of the Sikhs, Amritsar, is about 4,000 km (2,500 miles) to the northwest of Delhi, near the Pakistan border. Every day, thousands of pilgrims flock to the city's greatest shrine, the Golden Temple – "Harimandir Sahib" – the most important of all Sikh shrines. Founded by Guru Arjun Dev in the 16th century, it houses a copy of the holy book of the Sikhs, the Granth Sahib, or Adigrantha –"first book". Loudspeakers broadcast reli- gious chants from inside the temple, and the faithful read all day from their venerated book. In the evening, the book is carried in a solemn ceremony on a litter to a secondary temple, where it is kept overnight. The beat- ing of drums and the sounds of an organ create an atmosphere of intense spirituality. At night, the gilded façade is reflected in the temple lake of Amrit, named after the "nectar of immortality".

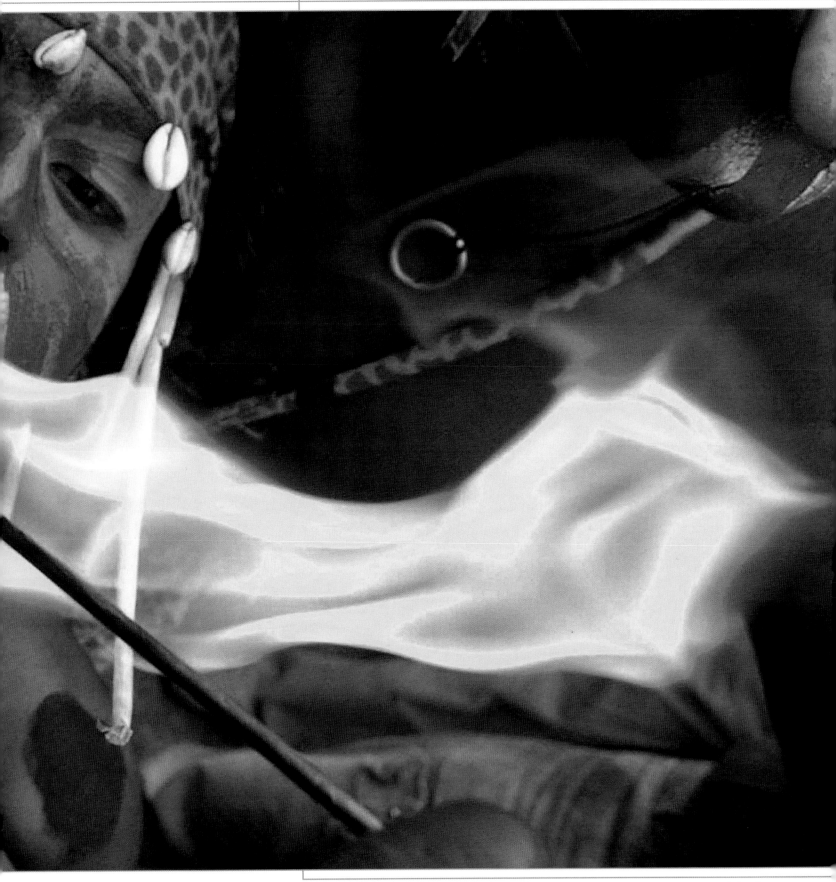

The holy book of the Sikhs in Amritsar (below, in the Golden Temple) contains roughly 6,000 hymns by various authors, mainly gurus, who were the first religious leaders of the community. Right: A worshipper in the temple complex.

SIKHS — THE TEACHINGS OF THE TWELVE GURUS

Guru Nanak Dev was born in 1469 in Talwandi, near Lahore, the present capital of Punjab, now part of Pakistan. Inspired by the Indian mystic and poet Kabir (1440–1518), Nanak at first led the life of a wandering religious teacher until, through his circle of disciples in Punjab, he became the founder of a reforming religion which combined elements of Hinduism (cycle of birth, karma, salvation through dedication to God) with central tenets of Islam (monotheism, ban on images). He died in Kartarpur (Punjab) around 1538. In the years that followed, nine successive gurus calling themselves Sikhs (students), expanded his teachings. In the face of external threat, the last guru, Gobind Singh (1666–1708), transformed the community into a tightly organized military fraternity, whose members were distinguished by their practice of wearing the "five Ks". These are the kirpan (a dagger), the kanga (a comb), the kara (an iron bracelet), the kaccha (short underwear), and kesh (hair of the head, uncut and worn under a turban, and untrimmed beard). These are the five attributes of all male Sikhs. Charity and service to neighbors have been prescribed since the time of the first guru. Every Sikh bears the second name "Singh" (lion) as a sign of bravery. Their most sacred shrine is the Harimandir Sahib, or Golden Temple, in Amritsar.

Delhi's bazaars are reminiscent of an Arabian souk, the sounds of traffic mixing with the calls of the sellers. Right: The India Gate is a victory arch in New Delhi designed by British architect Sir Edwin Landseer Lutyens (1869–1944).

Delhi

The cityscapes of Old and New Delhi are full of contrasts, but scattered throughout both are ancient monuments that stand as silent witnesses to a truly eventful history. Strictly speaking, Old Delhi comprises the former Shahjahanabad, the city founded by Mughal emperor Shah Jahan in the 17th century, which, with its labyrinthine alleyways in the bazaar quarter around the main commercial street of Chandni Chowk, still has a medieval feel to it. New Delhi to the south, by contrast, strikes a rather more imperial chord with broad, leafy avenues, green parks and grandiose buildings. Its design was entrusted to British architects Sir Edwin Lutyens and Hubert Baker. In 1931, after twenty years of construction, New Delhi was declared the capital of British India. By 1947, however, the situation had changed and New Delhi became the capital of the independent Republic of India (Bharat).

Enclosed by massive walls of red sandstone, the Red Fort is nearly a kilometer (1,090 yds) long and over 500 m (545 yds) wide. The complex has magnificent, marble-clad palaces and pavilions (below) from the Mughal era. Right: The Lahore Gate, the main entrance to the fortress.

The Red Fort in Delhi

Shah Jahan (Persian for "King of the World") was the fifth of the great Mughal rulers of India and an important commissioner of buildings – the Taj Mahal in Agra being the most famous example. It took nine years from 1639 to 1648 to complete a fortified palace located directly next to the older Muslim fortress of Salimgarh, constructed by Islam Shah Suri in 1546. Together, the ensemble of buildings forms the Red Fort of Old Delhi, whose name comes from the massive, 16-m-tall (52-ft) outer walls of red sandstone, which reflect a spectacular orange light during sunset. Despite repeated destruction over the centuries, the spacious Diwan-I-Am (public audience hall) with the imperial throne, the white marble Diwan-I-Khas (private audience hall), where the peacock throne once stood, and the intimate Moti Masjid (Pearl Mosque) of the Emperor Aurangzeb still remain.

Humayun's mausoleum, set amid gardens and designed by the Persian master architect Mirak Mirza Ghiya, became the model for many Mughal buildings. In the burial chamber (right), a white marble sarcophagus rests on a marble slab; the tomb itself is in a crypt below the chamber.

The Tomb of Humayun in Delhi

The first buildings to set the tone for Mughal architectural styles were those commissioned by Nasir ud-din Muhammad Humayun (1508–1556), born in Kabul to Babur, founder of the Mughal dynasty. Humayun's rule over India, which lasted from 1531 to 1556, was precarious at first, and he spent fifteen years exiled in Persia during that time. Upon his return, he brought an army not only of soldiers but also of builders and crafts-

men whose influences can be seen in the tomb's dome, which rests on a high drum. The arches are executed in Persian style. The use of white marble and red sandstone in the facade also allude to ancient Persian building traditions. The tomb of Humayun was constructed on the initiative of his wife, Haji Begum. The great Mughal died in 1556, but his remains only found their final resting place here in 1570.

The columns and ruins of this former mosque are richly ornamented. The 72-m-tall (238-ft) Qutb Minar (right) is the tallest brick minaret in the world, but it is structurally unstable and cannot be climbed. It is where the first Muslim kingdom was founded in northern India in the 12th century.

The Qutb complex in Delhi

From the beginning of the 13th to the 16th centuries, India was heavily influenced by the Delhi Sultanate, an Indian Muslim state from the pre-Mughal era that had been created by Qutb-ud-din Aybak, the general of the Turkish Sultanate of Afghanistan. Qutb-ud-din Aybak (1150–1210) is considered to be the founder of the "Slave Dynasty", so called because Qutb-ud-din Aybak was once the slave of the Muslim conqueror Muhammad Ghori, whom he murdered on the Indus in 1206. Under his successors, the domain of the Delhi Sultanate extended over nearly the entire subcontinent before it was finally conquered by Kabul's Mughal emperor Nasir ud-din Muhammad Humayun (1508–1556). Reminders of the Delhi Sultanate that can be seen today include India's oldest mosque, Quwwat-ul-Islam ("Might of Islam") and Qutb Minar, the victory minaret.

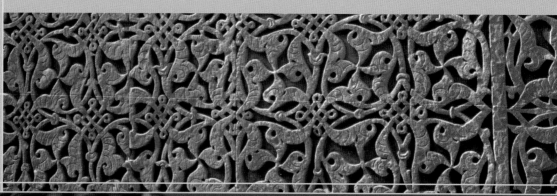

The Qutb Minar in Delhi is one of the most remarkable examples of the fusion of Indian and Islamic architecture. The innumerable variations on ornamental and geometric forms harken back to the architectural traditions of the Mughal conquerors.

TWO WORLDS INTERTWINED: INDO-ISLAMIC ARCHITECTURE

In Indian architecture of the Mughal era, the Hindu view of the world, which aims to unify humans and the cosmic order, meets with the demands of sacred and princely Islamic styles. In the 16th and 17th centuries, in the region between Lahore, Jaipur, Delhi and Agra (as well as in southern India) palaces, mosques and tombs of astounding beauty were built using both styles. During the 12th and 13th centuries, at the beginning of the Islamic conquest of India, it was enough to add Persian façades to Hindu temples, and "improve" their walls and columns with verses from the Koran. Hindu techniques were later combined with Persian-Islamic forms, which culminated in the playful imperial architecture of the classic Mughal period. The master builders of the emperors Babur, Akbar and Shah Jahan used red sandstone and white marble instead of Persian brick, and later added inlays of semi-precious stones. Among the most typical features are domes, onion-shaped and often of enormous scale, as seen in the Taj Mahal in Agra and Gol Gumbaz in Bijapur. Façades are divided by ogee (pointed) arches and niches. Multi-storied pavilions and slender minarets add accents, while interiors and courtyards along with symmetrical gardens exude an atmosphere of harmony and geometric perfection.

The Bahai Lotus Temple (below) was designed by Iranian architect Fariburz Sahba. Mahatma Gandhi consecrated the Lakshmi Narayan Temple (top right). Right: Actors impersonate Krishna and his wife Radha during the Janmashtami Festival, which celebrates Krishna's birth.

Lakshmi Narayan Temple and Bahai Lotus Temple in Delhi

The area around Connaught Place and along Janpath, New Delhi's main thoroughfare, is dominated by the hustle and bustle of business activity. In 1938, on the west side of Connaught Place, Indian industrial magnate B.D. Birla built the largest Hindu temple in the city – the Lakshmi-Narayan Temple, also referred to as the Birla Mandir Temple after its founder. The temple is dedicated to the divine couple Vishnu and Lakshmi. Its gingerbread decoration and colorful statues of the gods reflect the prevailing taste at that time. Much more modern – futuristic, even – is the Baha'i Lotus Temple, a white marble creation built by the Baha'i community, a religious group originally from Persia. Since 1986, this architectural marvel, a shrine in the shape of a lotus blossom, has been a place of pilgrimage for this humanitarian religious community.

The imperial architecture of Akbar is exemplified by the Amar Singh Gate and the outer fortifications of the Red Fort (below). In contrast, Shah Jahan preferred white marble (far right). The outer walls of the fort (right, with watchtowers) have a total length of 2.5 km (1.5 miles).

The Red Fort in Agra

The city of Agra lies on the west bank of the Yamuna River. It owes its importance to the Mughal emperors, in particular Akbar the Great (1542–1605), son of Humayan, who made the town the capital of his empire in 1568, and ordered the construction of the Red Fort. The project took nine years (1565–1574). His successors expanded the palace complex and made it into one of the largest fortresses in the world.

The 1-km-long (0.6-miles) outer wall once enclosed as many as 500 buildings. Particularly beautiful is the Palace of Emperor Jehangir in red sandstone. Shah Jahan, the greatest builder of the Mughal era, preferred the fine white marble of Makrana, in Rajasthan, to the local red sandstone. Precious inlay work is a feature of the octagonal Jasmine Tower (Saman Burj), where Shah Jahan lived under house arrest until his death.

"Love expressed in marble", "sighs turned to stone" – given its history and grandeur, it's no wonder the Taj Mahal inspires such poetic descriptions. Possibly the most beautiful words come from Nobel laureate Rabindranath Tagore: "a solitary teardrop on the cheek of time".

Taj Mahal in Agra

"Mumtaz Mahal" ("Chosen One of the Palace") was the name given by the Emperor Shah Jahan to his favorite wife, Arjumand Banu Begum, who after seventeen years of marriage died while giving birth to their fourteenth child in 1629. The emperor had a mausoleum built in her memory and named it the "Taj Mahal" ("Crown of the Palace"). Approximately 20,000 workers and artisans were involved in the construction, which lasted twenty-two years. The perfect harmony of the dazzling white dome is fully complemented by the symmetry of the garden canals and fountains. Four minaret-like towers create a frame for the seemingly weightless building. Pointed niches and marble reliefs adorn the façades. A monumental portal decorated with verses from the Koran leads to the interior, which contains the cenotaphs of the imperial couple.

The main chamber (below) of the Taj Mahal houses the cenotaphs, both empty, of Shah Jahan and his spouse (top: miniature portraits on ivory; the actual tombs are in the crypt beneath the chamber). The marble cenotaphs and walls are decorated with verses from the Koran and elaborate inlay work (right page).

THE MAGNIFICENT GRIEF OF THE GREAT MUGHAL SHAH JAHAN

His tears filled an entire lake, which today still reflects the silhouette of one of the greatest mausoleums in the world. The Taj Mahal is a shimmering white monument to the eternal mourning of the great Mughal emperor Shah Jahan over the death of his beloved wife. As a young prince, he had led his father's army on many success-ful campaigns, and yet after ascending the throne in 1628 the glory of battle appealed to him much less than did his appreciation of art and more refined pleasures. This did not prevent him, however, from establishing his claim to the throne by force, or making war to expand the Mughal empire, or sup-pressing Hinduism. He made good on the gains of his predecessors, especially his grandfather Akbar, who had politically con-solidated and economically strengthened the Mughal empire, not least through his religious tolerance. The court of Shah Jahan attained an opulence that had never been seen before. He ordered the construction of buildings that are among the masterpieces of Indo-Islamic architecture. The emperor died in 1666, with his final resting place at the side of his beloved wife. His plans for a black marble tomb to comple-ment his wife's was never realized. Eight years before his death in 1658, his third son Aurangzeb had already taken away his power and put him under house arrest.

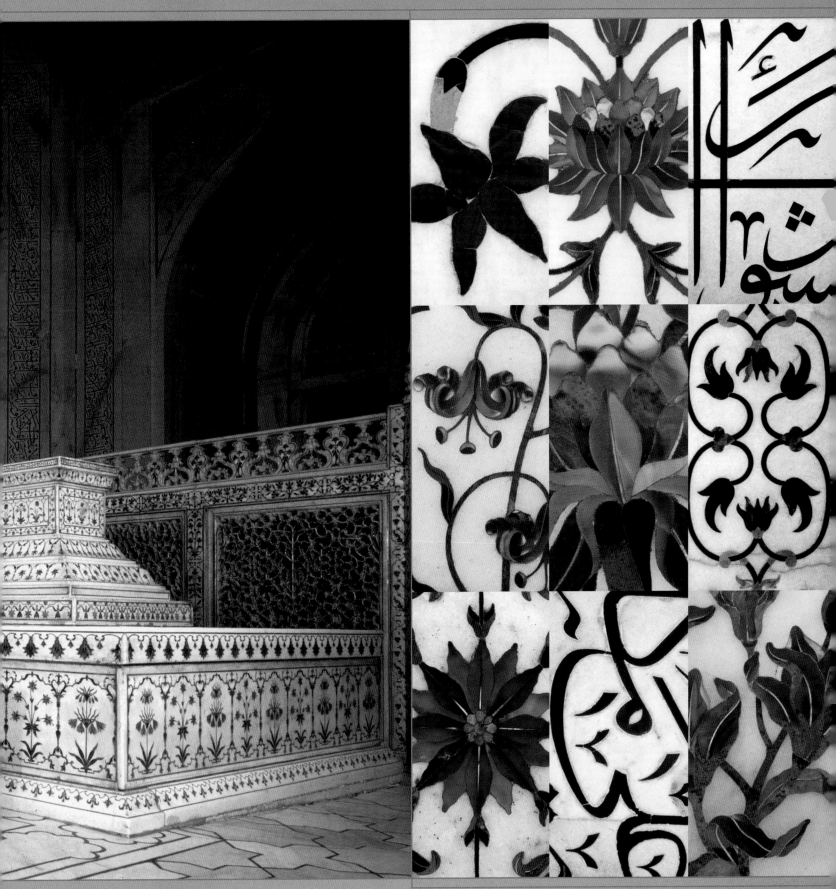

A "jewel box in marble" is how the mausoleum of Itimad-ud-Daulah has been described. The building in the center of a quiet garden on the banks of the Yamuna represents the shift from Akbar's red sandstone architecture to the elegant marble opulence of Shah Jahan's Taj Mahal.

The Mausoleum of Itimad-ud-Daulah in Agra

In the 17th century, Jahan, the Persian princess and favorite wife of the fourth Mughal emperor Jehangir, built a lasting monument to her father Mirza Ghiyas Beg, who had been given the title of Itimad-ud-Daulah for his service as the emperor's treasurer and grand vizier. The mausoleum could be described as a sumptuous jewel box in marble. The sarcophagi of Itimad-ud-Daulah and his wife Asmat-ul-Nissa are in the central chamber at platform level, with their cenotaphs directly over them under the folding roof. An extravagant abundance of multicolored, often inch-thick inlaid stones decorate the delicate marble edifice, which repeatedly features the Persian motif of the vase. The wall paintings in the side chambers are also worth viewing. The architecture and details are clearly recognizable as the work of Persian master craftsmen.

The south main gate of the complex (below) is a beautiful sandstone structure with an imposing central arch and a mosaic of white marble, black slate, and colored stone. You pass through the gate into the gardens and towards the main portion of the mausoleum (right).

Akbar Mausoleum in Sikandra

Construction of Akbar the Great's tomb began during his lifetime in a small town on the outskirts of Agra. Allegedly, he designed the building – which looks more like a palace than a mausoleum – and also oversaw the construction work himself. In any case, it was not completed until 1613, under the auspices of his son Jehangir (1569–1627). Akbar's tomb deviates in many ways from classic Islamic architectural tradition. There are none of the onion domes that are typical of mausoleums of the Mughal period. Instead, the three-storied recessed structure features a roof with an open courtyard, which is enclosed by a marble screen. The rooms on the ground floor are decorated with exquisitely intricate murals. Much of the paint used for them was made from ground semi-precious stones such as lapis lazuli.

Right: The inner courtyard of the Great Mosque. Inset below: The mausoleum of Shaikh Salim. Muslims pray alongside Sufis here – Salim was a follower of Sufism. The interior of the mosque is notable for its sumptuous decoration (far right).

Fatehpur Sikri

In 1569, Akbar moved the capital of his empire from Agra to Sikri twenty-five miles away. It was the home of the hermit Salim Chishti, who had prophesied the birth of an heir to the throne. After the prophecy had been fulfilled, the emperor ordered construction of a splendid new capital on the site that had augured so well for him. He named the city Fatehpur ("City of Victory"). Of particular interest to visitors are the private audience hall with its central column where the throne was placed, the spacious courtyard where Akbar indulged in chess using living figures, the Panch Mahal (a five-story sandstone pavilion), and the delightful palace of the Turkish princess Rumi Sultana. The mosque features the tomb of the Sufi saint Salim Chishti in white marble, sumptuous screen windows and the imposing Buland Darwaza ("Gate of Magnificence").

"We have the rainforests of the Amazon to provide oxygen for the planet. And to provide for the soul of our planet, we have India" – Salman Rushdie. Below and right: Allahabad pilgrimage site. Far left, from top: Haridwar, Nasik and Ujjain.

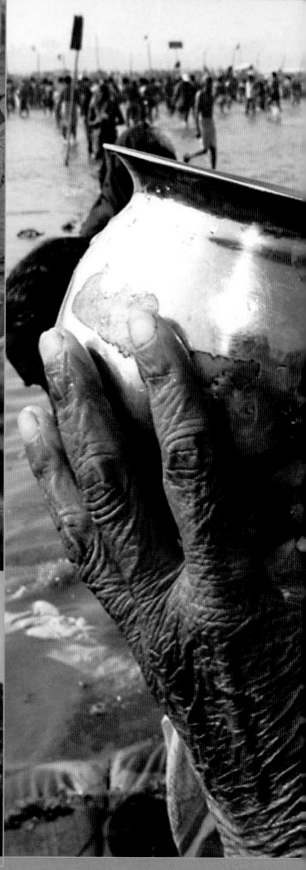

THE WORLD'S LARGEST RELIGIOUS FESTIVAL: MAHA KUMBH MELA

Long ago, the Hindu gods and demons fought over the amrita, the "nectar of immortality". The nectar was being kept in a pitcher ("kumbh"), from which four drops fell during a twelve-day battle for its possession. The spots on Earth where the drops fell – Allahabad, Nashik, Ujjain, and Haridwar – have been holy places for Hin-dus ever since, and every twelve years a great ("maha") festival ("mela") takes place: the Maha Kumbh Mela, or "Great Festival of the Pitcher". During the festival, Brahmin priests, holy men in saffron robes, naked yogis, and the faithful from all levels of society meet for ritual bathing in the sin-cleansing waters, the most "purifying" of which are said to be in Allahabad. This is because Allahabad is also the place where the Yamuna and Ganges rivers meet the sacred Sarasvati, an invisible, subterranean river mentioned in Hindu mythology. Thus, the city formerly known as Prayag, which was renamed Allahabad ("City of Allah") by Akbar the Great in 1575, is not only one of the oldest places of pilgrimage in India, it's also one of the holiest. At the last Kumbh Mela in Allahabad (in 2001) an estimated thirty million pilgrims came for the ritual bathing at the confluence of the three rivers ("Triveni"). Other festivals took place in Nashik in 2003, and in Ujjain in 2004.

Varanasi is the holiest city in the Hindu realm. Many of the faithful come not only to purify themselves in the Ganges, but also to die here. It is said that here Shiva whispers into the ear of the dying, and whoever dies in Varanasi, the "City of Light", is assured liberation.

Varanasi

In ancient times, Varanasi was part of the kingdom of Kashi. It has been mentioned as a place of Hindu pilgrimage since the seventh century and most of its temples are dedicated to Shiva. Every day, pilgrims from around the world stream into the city, take a ritual bath of purification in the Ganges, walk from temple to temple, and pour Ganges water over the lingam, the phallic symbol of Shiva. Every practicing Hindu should make the pilgrimage to Varanasi (formerly Benares) once in a lifetime to ensure a better reincarnation, or to free the soul from the cycle of reincarnation. The bathing ghats, or stations, are especially lively early in the morning when the sun rises over the horizon. Religious music emanates from the temples, the faithful dip their prayers into the cloudy waters, and offerings of orange marigold garlands and oil lamps are made to the sacred river.

In India, people who have dedicated their lives to religion (right, in Varanasi) express their devotion to a deity by wearing a "tilaka" – a divine mark on the forehead (below). The forehead, free of any bodily secretions, is for Hindus a particularly clean part of the body. The ritual markings are deeply symbolic. For example, three horizontal lines drawn across the forehead symbolize Shiva's three eyes, while a U-shaped emblem with a central vertical line symbolizes the three steps that Vishna took when he measured the universe, growing at the same time from a dwarf to a giant.

SADHUS: INDIA'S HOLY MEN

The holy men of India are recognizable from a distance with their saffron-tinted robes, matted hair, walking sticks and begging bowls. Some sadhus live as hermits in forests and caves while others wander throughout the land as ascetics and preachers. Holy men often sink into a state of meditation for months at a time or, as a sign of retreat from worldly life, they cast off all their clothes. They smear their bodies with ashes taken from funeral pyres as a reminder of the transitory nature of life. They express their veneration for a deity by painting a divine symbol on their foreheads. The forehead, it is said, is unsullied by bodily excretions and thus considered by Hindus to be a particularly pure part of the body. Followers of Vishnu paint a U-shaped emblem with a stripe down the middle, which symbolizes his three steps: according to tradition, Vishnu walked across the universe in three steps while growing from a dwarf into a giant. These three steps are a symbol for sunrise, zenith and sunset, and are interpreted as taking possession of the cosmos. Followers of Shiva, on the other hand, paint three horizontal white lines across their foreheads to symbolize the three eyes of their god. The popular red dot in the center of the forehead is another symbol of the mystical eye of wisdom.

Below: A wall painting in the Mahabodhi Temple in Bodh Gaya shows demons attacking the Buddha in an attempt to prevent his enlightenment. The temple tower, adorned with sculptures, soars into the sky like a pyramid (right). Inside is a gilded statue of the Buddha.

Mahabodhi Temple in Bodh Gaya

The first large-scale and centrally-governed empire in the history of India, which included large parts of the Indian subcontinent and extended to present-day Afghanistan, was founded by King Ashoka in 272 BC. He had converted to Buddhism when he ordered the construction of a temple on the site of the Mahabodhi tree in Bodh Gaya, under which the Buddha had attained his divine enlightenment. The present building, which rises to about 50 m (180 ft), was built during the Gupta Dynasty (AD 320–540), which adopted Buddhism as the official religion. Mahabodhi Temple is not only a symbol of great national and spiritual power: as one of the oldest brick temple towers on the subcontinent, it also has a special significance in the architectural history of India. Its stone reliefs and the sculpted decoration of its balustrades are particularly impressive.

This guard at the Junagarh Fort in Bikaner twirls his moustache in a show of pride. Bikaner was once one of the three great desert states of Rajasthan, along with Jodhpur and Jaisalmer.

Situated in the heart of Jaipur, the City Palace was the residence of the ruling family as far back as the early 18th century Below: The audience hall, still used by the Maharaja.

JAIPUR AND THE NORTH-WEST

The border between India and Pakistan runs over 960 km (600 mi) through the Thar, a desert of salt, rock and sand in the north-west of India. This inhospitable zone has been inhabited for more than five thousand years, as evidenced by archaeological finds dating to the era of the Indus Valley cultures. The Aravalli Range separates the desolate north from the grasslands and agricultural landscapes of the east and south. The clothing of the people of Rajasthan, a riot of brilliant colors, is quite striking.

The art of turning a simple piece of cloth into a beautiful garment, be it an elegantly draped sari, a woman's traditional headscarf, or a man's perfectly shaped turban, is highly developed throughout India. But nowhere else are the dyes used for them as sumptuous as in Rajasthan.

THE LAND OF PRINCES AND POTENTATES

The noble Rajputs (from the Sanskrit: "sons of kings") have always represented the dominant social class of north-west India. They trace their elite status from the sun, moon and fire, the nature gods of Hinduism. The Rajputs eventually became the most zealous defenders of the Hindu faith, and in the Middle Ages they fought chivalrously against their Muslim conquerors from Central Asia. Some of the approximately thirty ruling dynasties were prepared to make political compromises with the Mogul emperors and later the British, and were thus able to hold on to their lands. Various marriages between Hindu dynastic houses and the imperial Mughal court also proved to be strategically opportune, and ultimately spared some of their holdings from the ravages of war. For over a thousand years, the Rajputs determined the fortunes of the Rajputana states, which were incorporated into the federal state of Rajasthan ("Land of Princes") after Indian independence. Nowadays, what remains of their opulent past are majestic castles and fairy-tale palaces. The old days come back to life during Hindu festivals, when maharajas, in the role of god-kings, appear in ceremonial garb complete with turbans and sabers and perform religious rituals under the direction of court Brahmins.

The most beautiful wall paintings in Shekhawati are found in two remote villages: Nawalgar (main photo and right) and in Mandawa (far right). Originally, they were painted by applying mainly vegetable dyes to the still wet masonry.

Shekhawati

The grassland region of Shekhawati lies in north-eastern Rajasthan and rose to fame through the extraordinary wall paintings and frescoes found in many of its noble manors. The southern route of the Silk Road ran through here. Caravans brought riches to the isolation and filled the purses of traders, who then displayed their wealth through lavish wall paintings on the façades and in the courtyards of their great mansions. What is most striking about the paintings dating from the late 18th to the early 20th centuries is the integration of modern themes into traditional art. The painting is still executed in the one-dimensional realism of the traditional Rajput style, but suddenly, from among the proud hunters and warriors, motifs from the British colonial era appear in the works. There is even an image of Krishna sitting in a Rolls Royce…

Right: The Thar Desert covers more than half of the state of Rajasthan, roughly 250,000 sq m (100,000 sq miles). The city of Jaisalmer (below with the temple lake, and inset bottom right) grew rich through trade from the caravan routes.
Inset: The necropolis of Bada Bagh.

The Thar Desert, Jaisalmer, Bada Bagh

For some travelers, the most impressive moment of a journey through Rajasthan comes after crossing the sandy expanse of the Thar desert and the honey-gold walls of Jaisalmer appear. Since the 12th century, these fortifications have dominated this hill town, where spice and silk merchant caravans passed through until well into the 19th century. But the opening of the Suez Canal brought a change in trade routes, specifically more sea trade, and Jaisalmer's great houses fell into decay. After the separation of Pakistan from India in 1947, Jaisalmer gained military significance due to its location near the western border, and became a center of Indian desert tourism.

The name "Bada Bagh", or "big garden", refers to a small hill oasis near Jaisalmer where you can visit some exquisite tombs.

Below: Ganesh Pol, the three-storied gate from 1640, leads to the private apartments of the fortress (right). Far right: Women lived on the upper floors, hidden behind grillwork windows. Bottom: The Jal Mahal, or "Water Palace", in Man Sagar Lake with its elegant dome towers.

The Fort Palace of Amber, The Jal Mahal Water Palace

Until 1727, the fort palace of Amber was the seat of the Kachhawa Dynasty, a fierce and proud Rajput clan of Hindus who belonged to the second-highest Indian caste reserved for warriors, princes and kings – the Kshatriya caste. The fortress was commissioned and built by Man Singh I (1540–164) in 1592, on the remains of an earlier structure dating from the 12th century. The lavish building in the middle of the complex was erected by Jai Singh I (1611–1667). It's possible to ride on the back of an elephant up the winding trails that lead to the mountain ridge where the palaces situated. The entrance to the fortress itself leads through the Suraj Pol, or Sun Gate. On the route to Jaipur there is another place of interest, the Jal Mahal, or Water Palace. During monsoon season, when the water level rises, the palace appears to be floating on Man Sagar Lake.

The oriel windows of the Palace of the Winds, adorned with stone lattices, allowed ladies of the court to observe the street without being seen (main photo). Inset: The observatory of Sawai Jai Singh II. Right: A market woman, a snake charmer, and an elephant driver.

Jaipur

The pink-colored façades of many buildings here have given Jaipur the nickname "Pink City". The capital of Rajasthan was founded in 1727, by Maharaja Sawai Jai Singh II (1688–1743), who has entered the annals of his country as a statesman, scholar, and patron of the arts. "Sawai" ("one and a quarter", i.e., more capable than ordinary men) is the honorary title given to outstanding persons and was bestowed on the maharaja by the Mughal emperor early in his forty-three-year reign. The city is divided into nine rectangular sectors enclosed within crenelated walls with seven gates. The streets are laid out in a checkerboard pattern. Among the principal attractions are the city palace of the maharaja, his observatory (Jantar Mantar), the Palace of the Winds (Hawa Mahal) with its striking, arched façade, and the lively Johari Bazaar.

Below: Hundreds of thousands of people pour into town for the Pushkar Mela bazaar, turning the otherwise rather sleepy place into one of the world's largest livestock markets – and the world's largest camel fair. A highlight for pilgrims is a dip in the holy lake (right).

Pushkar

Agra, Jaipur and the nearby national parks attract more visitors than even the ancient royal capital of Alwar, which is mentioned in India's great Mahabharata epic from the 2nd century BC. And the atmosphere of the city is actually all the more authentic for it. The Rajput palace is surrounded by gardens, but most of its rooms are filled to the rafters with piles of documents from various government offices. The museum on the fifth floor features hunting trophies and silver tables, yard-long painted scrolls and various works from the Bundi school of painting.

Jaipur's mountainous surroundings also offer palaces, idyllic gardens, forts and temple complexes such as the sacred reservoirs near the Surya temple in the Galta Valley, or the marble tombs of the Kachhawa kings in Gaitor, in an open garden on the road to Amber.

Below: The 19th-century City Palace of Alwar rises over the temple pond. Far right: The reservoirs below the Surya Temple in the Galta Valley are fed by springs said to have healing properties. Right: The royal tomb of Gaitor.

Alwar, Galta, Gaitor

Agra, Jaipur and the nearby national parks attract more visitors than even the ancient royal capital of Alwar, which is mentioned in India's great Mahabharata epic from the 2nd century BC. And the atmosphere of the city is actually all the more authentic for it. The Rajput palace is surrounded by gardens, but most of its rooms are filled to the rafters with piles of documents from various government offices. The museum on the fifth floor features hunting trophies and silver tables, yard-long painted scrolls and various works from the Bundi school of painting.

Jaipur's mountainous surroundings also offer palaces, idyllic gardens, forts and temple complexes such as the sacred reservoirs near the Surya temple in the Galta Valley, or the marble tombs of the Kachhawa kings in Gaitor, in an open garden on the road to Amber.

Jaipur is one of the most important centers of jewelry production in India and the art of working gold and silver (below) is passed down from generation to generation. The city is also famous for its kundan-kari: setting precious stones in gold and silver. Right: A tourmaline polished as a cabochon.

TRADITIONAL HANDICRAFTS IN RAJASTHAN

Under its princely patronage, Rajasthan became a center for myriad types of handicrafts. A good example would be the heavy silver ornaments made here: arm and leg bracelets are still produced according to traditional methods, as are the filigreed nose and toe rings. Another regional specialty of Jaipur is enameled jewelry (meenakari), which is sometimes set with precious stones (kundankari).

Handicrafts particular to Rajasthan include Pichwai, religious paintings on silk or cloth wall hangings that show scenes from the life of Krishna. Phad paintings made on linen are also typical of the area, with depictions of legendary heroes.

The courtly art of miniature painting, which originally came from Persia, also survives today in Rajasthan, as does the production of white-blue turquoise ceramics. Favorite motifs for these exquisite miniatures include hunting, deities, religious festivals and illustrations of everyday life at court.

The chief industry in Jaipur is precious stone cutting, especially emeralds and diamonds from Africa, South America, and India. Hand-printed textiles and cashmere shawls of varying quality are also produced here. Traditional Bandhani fabrics are made by tying knots in the material before it is soaked in dye

The semi-man-made wetlands of the Keoladeo National Park cover a mere 30 sq km (11.5 sq miles), but they are a refuge for the purple heron (main photo), the Indian roller, the ring-necked (or rose-ringed) parakeet and the kingfisher (inserts, from left).

Keoladeo National Park

This national park is a wetlands that resulted from human development. The area used to be the hunting grounds of the maharajas of Bharatpur, as the swampy lowland was home to wild ducks. Indeed, it was not uncommon to bag several thousand birds during a day's hunt. In the 19th century, the maharajas ordered construction of canals and dams in order to expand the flooded areas. Thus, a landscape was created that soon became a favorite breeding ground for all kinds of birds since the surrounding region is actually very dry. Today, the nature reserve offers a year-round home to about 120 species of birds, among them herons, whose population here is one of the largest in the world. It is also the winter home for about 240 species of migratory birds, including the rare Siberian crane (also known as the snow crane) and the falcated duck.

In the Hindu world, blue is a divine color. For this reason, only the houses of Brahmins, the highest Hindu caste, were painted blue in Jodhpur. The Mehranghar Fort of the Rathore rulers towers 120 m (400 ft) above the Old Town.

Jodhpur

The Mehrangarh Fort here towers majestically over the city. Splendid buildings such as the Moti Mahal (Palace of Pearls) and the Phool Mahal (Palace of Flowers) from the 16th to 19th centuries contain lavish wall paintings, stained glass windows, and mirror work reminiscent of the opulent lifestyle of the Rathore maharajas. In 1459, Rathore King Rao Jodha (1416–1484) chose a prominent crag for the construction of his fortress. The city of Jodhpur, named after him, spreads out below with its famous blue Brahmin houses. The Umaid-Bhawan Palace, begun in 1929, belongs to Maharaja Gaj Singh II, the present head of the Rathore Dynasty and one of the best-known members of Indian royalty both home and abroad. One half of the palace is a luxury hotel and museum, while the other half serves as the home of Gaj Singh II (born in 1948) and his family.

Below: Udaipur is a city adorned with many wall paintings. It is also called the "Queen of the Lakes". Top left: The Jag Niwas lake palace (below) was once a James Bond film set. Top right and middle: The City Palace (inset) of the Maharanas of Mewar is still the family residence.

Udaipur

The lakes and marble palaces of Udaipur give the city a fairy-tale aura. Nestled into the Aravalli Hills, the Old Town enchants visitors with its houses and traditional wall paintings. Udaipur was founded by Maharana Udai Singh (1522–1572) in 1559, a Rajput of the Sisoida clan, whose roots can be traced back to the year 566. The city palace on Lake Pichola dates from the founding years of the 16th century, while Jag Niwas, the Lake Palace, was built in the 18th century as the summer residence of the royal family. Today, it functions as a hotel, as does the lovely island palace Jag Mandir, built in 1620, which has an entrance guarded by eight stone elephants. This was where the later Mughal ruler Shah Jahan once took refuge in 1626, while hiding from his father before carrying out the rebellion he was planning against him.

Below: A monument in Delhi commemorates Gandhi's legendary "Salt March" in March, 1930, when he and some of his loyal followers walked 385 km (240 miles) from his ashram near Ahmedabad to the Arabian Sea in twenty-four days. The aim of the campaign was a symbolic gesture: to produce a few grains of salt from the ocean in order to demonstrate a form of civil disobedience as salt manufacture was reserved for the British. In Delhi you can also visit the National Gandhi Museum, which houses the workroom of this dedicated pacifist (facing page). Right: These photos show him as a law student in 1887, a lawyer in Durban, South Africa, in 1900, and six years before India's independence in 1941.

A GREAT SOUL: MAHATMA GANDHI

Born on October 2, 1869, in Porbandar on the west coast of Gujarat, Mohandas Karamchand – called Mahatma – Gandhi established himself later as a lawyer in Bombay after completing his law studies in London. In 1893, he moved to Durban, South Africa, to work as a legal advisor for an Indian company, and ended up staying in the country for twenty years fighting colonial discrimination against Indians. He returned to India in 1914, and began working for home rule in India. His policy of non-violent struggle, passive resistance, refusal to cooperate with the authorities, and his call for the boycott of British products caused a sensation around the world. Gandhi, whose life had been dictated by prayer, fasting, renunciation and meditation was treated as a national hero by the Indian people, who gave him the honorary title of "Mahatma" (from the Sanskrit: "great soul"). He used all his resources to prevent the partition of the subcontinent into an Islamic Pakistan and a secular India, striving instead to bring Hindus and Muslims together, despite repeated setbacks. All was ultimately in vain: India became independent at midnight on August 15, 1947, but the subcontinent was partitioned. Gandhi was assassinated by a Hindu fanatic on January 30, 1948, on his way to evening prayer.

Inset: The "Gateway of India, a Mumbai landmark seen here at sunset, was designed by Scotsman George Wittet and completed in 1924. It stands in the Colaba quarter of the city.

Like no other edifice in the city, the Chhatrapati Shivaji Terminus in Mumbai unites the Indian style elements of British Gothic Revival with traditional Indian palace architecture.

MUMBAI, GOA AND CENTRAL INDIA

Imposing isolated mountains of granite and gneiss punctuate the archaic landscape of the Deccan Plateau in the heart of India. Thick jungles cover the mountains of the western Ghats, which descend to the Arabian Sea in steep steps. The heartland of the subcontinent has a rich cultural landscape. The highland plains are home to precious treasures, such as the country's oldest Hindu temple, in Pattadakal, or the over two thousand-year-old Buddhist shrine in Sanchi. Mumbai and Goa are provide contrast on the west coast.

Realistic detail and vitality are the hallmarks of the images carved in stone on the temple of Khajuraho. The erotic motifs are the visual symbols of the eternal cycle of creation and dissolution. Of the once eighty temples here, only twenty-two remain.

Khajuraho

Khajuraho can be divided into sections. In the village itself is a group of temples dedicated to Brahma, Vamana and Javari. The Jain temples are located to the east and are today still centers of active devotion. Khajuraho was the capital of the Chandela kings in the 10th and 11th centuries, as seen in the temples to Lakshmana, Kandariya, Vishvanath, and Chitragupta. Each of these is oriented from east to west. At the western end is the entrance hall; after that come the porch, assembly hall, vestibule and inner sanctum. The tower-like roofs atop the individual elements rise progressively higher towards the sanctum, which symbolizes Mount Meru at the center of the world – the home of the gods – and houses the image of the deity, which faces east. Sexual acts depicted in the temples symbolize fertility and the regeneration of the world.

One of the orders of Jainism is the Digambara (from the Sanskrit: sky-clad). Below: Monks in front of the statue of Gomatheswara in Sravana Belagola. Right: The temple of Ranakpur, one of the five holiest shrines of Jainism. Each one of the hundreds of stone columns and domes is individually carved.

In the 6th century BC, Mahavira, the founder of Jainism, was among the people preaching "ahimsa", a doctrine of absolute non-violence akin to the tenets of Buddhism. Twenty-two "tirthankaras", or prophets, served as role models of this religious code, but only the last one, Mahavira the Reformer, who was a contemporary of the Buddha, is an actual historical figure. He is often represented as a naked ascetic with a lion as his emblem. According to Jain beliefs, the world is ruled not by one god, but by cosmic and ethical laws. The soul, which is eternal and encased in a material body, commits good or bad deeds in its wanderings as a transitory deity, human being, animal, or demon. Salvation exists only after the soul has freed itself of all material things, a state that can only be attained after countless rebirths and through ethical behavior, asceticism and meditation. The mastery over body and soul through asceticism and meditation makes a person into a "jina", a conqueror of passion and desire, to whom salvation from the cycle of rebirths is assured. In India, there are about four million Jains. Since they cannot reconcile many occupations with their beliefs, they practice mainly academic and commercial professions. As a wealthy and influential minority, they belong to the economic elite of India.

Below: Impressive relief carvings adorn the stone gates of the stupas of Sanchi. The scenes are mostly from the life of the Buddha (right). Only ruins remain of the other temples at the pilgrimage site, an important religious center well into the 12th century.

Sanchi

Sanchi, located to the north-east of Bhopal in the state of Madhya Pradesh, is an important pilgrimage destination and the oldest Buddhist shrine in India. According to lore, the Great Stupa temple complex was built by King Ashoka the Great (268–233 BBC), an avid supporter of Buddhism. Indeed, according to the ruins excavated and restored between 1912 and 1919, a few of the buildings can definitely be attributed to him.

The highest degree of craftsmanship is displayed in the splendid stonemasonry of the larger stupa, erected in the middle of the third century BC over the bones of the Buddha, as legend has it. The hemispherical sanctuary is surrounded by a stone balustrade with four monumental gateways (toranas) aligned with the four points of the compass. These were all constructed in the 1st century BC.

Below: The magnificently decorated cave temples of Ajanta are as impressive as any outdoor temple complexes. Right: Eight of the caves have restored wall paintings that are quite extraordinary in their narrative depth and artistic design.

Ajanta

The Buddhist cave temples of Ajanta had long fallen into obscurity when they were rediscovered by British officers in 1819. They are located about 100 km (60 miles) north of Aurangabad in a ravine on a curve in the Waghora River in the state of Maharashtra. During two phases of construction, Buddhist monks cut twenty-nine caves into the nearly vertical rock face. The first construction phase comprised the period between the 2nd century BC and the 2nd century AD. The second phase took place between the 5th and 6th centuries. Eight caves in this magnificent complex have wall paintings that are still intact and show an extraordinary richness of narrative and artistic composition. They depict scenes from the life of the Buddha and Jataka tales, stories and legends about the Buddha's previous incarnations.

Below: The Kailash Temple is the largest rock sanctuary in Ellora. The image of Buddha, sitting under the mahabodi – or banyan – tree (right) is found repeatedly in the temple. It was under such a tree that the Buddha is said to have achieved enlightenment.

Ellora

The Maharashtra Plateau, with its canyons cut deep in the basalt rock, proved from a geological point of view to be especially well suited for the construction of monolithic cliff temples. The common feature of all the Ellora shrines is that they were hewn out of the rock, and not built into it. Meaning, the essential load-bearing architectural elements are all part of the solid rock. This is also true for most of the architectural ornamentation and many of the sculptures. Each temple consists of an entry hall, a porch, a main hall and an inner sanctum. The latter houses a sculpture of a deity – hence the highest ceiling – that depicts the sacred world mountain Meru, a typical motif in India. In the Kailash Temple – the largest cave shrine in Ellora, and one that imitates a free-standing building – the roof of the sanctum represents the holy mountain Kailash, the home of the god Shiva.

Below: The only thing to do is move out of the way when a holy cow blocks the chaotic traffic in Mumbai. Facing page: Two Indian navy cadets at Victoria Terminal, a symbol of British colonial rule in Mumbai like the India Gate victory arch (right).

Mumbai

Mumbai, formerly Bombay, is a city of superlatives in the 21st century. The city originally gained importance due to its protected bay, the East India Company, and the Parsi people. Its transformation from a fishing village to the largest economic center in South Asia with seventeen million inhabitants was rapid. In 1661, the Portuguese settlement was transferred to Britain as a dowry for Catherine of Braganza when she married King Charles II. In the 19th century, Bombay became India's most important city for textiles. The first university was opened in 1857, and the first train departed from Victoria Terminus in 1860. Today, the splendid colonial buildings are fading in the shadow of ever taller office and residential towers. It is India's richest city, an economic powerhouse and financial center, and the world's largest film production center, Bollywood.

Below: Ellora Arts is one of Mumbai's largest poster studios. As many as 250 Hindi films are made each year in Mumbai in studios such as Filmalaya (right). Megastar Amitabh Bachchan (inset, far right, 2nd from top) is known as the undisputed "King of Indian film".

BOLLYWOOD: STRONG HEROES, BEAUTIFUL WOMEN

When it comes to Indian films, it's all in the recipe. "Hindi masala" is what Indians call mainstream movies, a "spicy stew" that gets its taste from just the right blend of the finest ingredients: music, dancing, romance and maybe even a bit of violence. Everything is loud and lively in typical Bollywood movies, and there is not much room for subtlety. The invariably masculine hero is proud and strong, the classically beautiful woman is weak and desirable and in the end, of course, they're happily united. The closing scenes in many of these movies are a riotously happy wedding, but few Indian filmmakers are interested in what happens afterwards. Modern phenomena such as DINK (double income, no kids) or DINS (double income, no sex) are being confronted only gradually as they become an increasing reality in the big cities along with rising divorce rates. Most of the economic success here is generated with Hindi language feature films, popularly known as "Bollywood" films, a name for India's film industry taken from a combination of Bombay (the former name for Mumbai) and Hollywood, even though films made in Hindi actually only account for a third of total Indian production, which also of course includes films in languages such as Tamil and Telugu.

All pictures: On an island in the bay off Mumbai, the cave temple dedicated to Shiva is famous above all for the stone carvings showing the deity in different poses and scenes with his three faces as creator, maintainer and destroyer.

Elephanta

Only an hour's boat ride separates Mumbai from idyllic Elephanta Island, home to a 7th-century cave temple dedicated to Shiva tucked away in the lush jungle. Together with Brahma and Vishnu, Shiva is one of the most important deities in the Hindu pantheon. A series of very impressive high-relief sculptures displays the various manifestations of Shiva – from the cosmic dancer Nataraja to the meditating ascetic Yogishwara.

On the front end of the cave, the three faces of Shiva emerge from the darkness. This image of the god as creator, maintainer, and destroyer is one of the most exalted works of art in the temple.

The deity also often appears with an entourage of creatures of a half-divine, half-demonic nature. Like Shiva, these cohorts have found an appropriate medium in the carvings of Elephanta.

The Virupaksha Temple, dedicated to Shiva, is the largest building in Pattadakal and has exquisite stone carvings (right). Nandi, or "the happy one", is the bull on which Shiva rides. In Hindu mythology, Nandi is Shiva's faithful servant and leader of his heavenly entourage.

Pattadakal

The Hindu temple complex of Pattadakal is situated in the western Deccan Plateau in a landscape known as "Karnata desa" or "black earth". In the 6th century, the Chalukya dynasty emerged as the major power in India. Prince Pulakesi I was the dynasty's founder, but it did not reach its zenith of power until Pulakesi II, who ruled between 609 and 642. Its location in the border area between northern and southern India in the present-day state of Karnataka, and the tolerance of the Chalukya rulers, made Pattadakal a melting pot for a variety of architectural styles. Nowhere else can one find the northern and southern Indian temple styles so closely juxtaposed. The northern Indian temple tower, or "nagara", has a convex, outward curving form, while the southern Indian "vimana" tapers in steps towards the top.

The cloister of Saint Francis of Assisi was a mosque before the Portuguese came. The ceiling of the cloister church is richly decorated (right). Below: During a long walk on the beach you can look for all kinds of interesting articles in the enormous fishing nets that are laid out to dry.

Goa

This small state on the west coast was a Portuguese colony until December 1961 – the last bastion of European power in India. The Catholic enclave was founded as far back as 1510 by Alfonso de Albuquerque (1453–1515). Old Goa (Velha Goa) is situated about 10 km (6 miles) inland and was abandoned early in the 19th century due to rampant malaria. A new city was built downstream, although the old churches and monasteries were not abandoned. They can still be seen in all their grandeur. The church of St Francis dates back to 1521. The Sé (cathedral) goes back to 1562 and was for a time the largest church in Asia. The most important mission church was erected here in 1594 – the basilica of Bom Jesu, which contains the tomb of St Francis Xavier (1506–1552), the Jesuit who brought Christianity to India and Japan.

Below: The former city of Vijayanagar is more or less an open-air museum for south Indian architecture. The large carriage in the temple area (right) is cut from a single block of stone. The temples are rich in reliefs and sculptures (top center and right). Far right: The Vitthala Temple

Hampi

The ruins of Hampi, the capital of Vijayanagar, the last great Hindu kingdom (1136–1565), are situated near the town of Hosapete in Central India. The temple area covers roughly 26 sq km (10 sq mi) and is surrounded by a breathtaking granite landscape strewn with boulders. The 50-m (162-ft) gateway leading to the Virupaksha Temple can be seen for miles around. Its inner sanctum is dedicated to Vishnu. Delicate stone carvings adorn the Vaishnavite Vitthala Temple, with its stone temple carriage for Garuda, a mythical bird-like creature. The monolith of Vishnu as man-lion in the Narasimha Temple was created during the reign of King Krishna Deva Raya (c. 1528), as was the Hazara Rama Temple with its fine reliefs. The largely destroyed palace district surprises with the Lotus Mahal, a pavilion with excellent stucco decoration in an Indo-Islamic style.

A sadhu in front of a shrine near the Tungabhadra River in Karnataka: "He who has been to India not only with his eyes, but with his soul, will always be homesick for it" – Hermann Hesse.

After a long period under threat of extinction the number of Royal Bengal tigers in the wild has risen thanks to strict protective measures. In India, the cat is considered the "King of the Jungle".

KOLKATA AND THE EAST

The Brahmaputra and the Ganges flow from the Himalayas and meander through the flat-lands of north-east India feeding fertile alluvial plains. Lush green rice and tea plantations define the landscape of Assam. The agricultural state of West Bengal is densely populated: The metropolitan area of Kolkata has more than thirteen million people. Orissa, on the Bay of Bengal, has gentle, palm-strewn landscapes that resemble southern India and possess a wealth of magnificent temples.

Langurs belong to the colobinae sub-family of monkeys. The Manas Game Reserve is home to the golden langur and the capped langur (below, left and right). The Indian elephant population is also on the rise again. Right: Two bull elephants duelling.

Manas Game Reserve

This game reserve, created in 1928, forms the core of the Manas National Park and was badly damaged by the civil unrest of 1992, during which only a few dozen of the remaining two thousand elephants living here survived. However, following a restocking program the number had risen to seven hundred by 2006. The population of the mighty Bengal tiger also grew to about sixty, but the rare Indian – or great one-horned – rhinoceros unfortunately died out in the Manas. In 2006, a relocation project began with animals taken from other parks. On the other hand, some animals thought to be extinct in Assam were discovered in the grasslands that make up about 60 percent of the Manas territory, including wild water buffaloes and pygmy hogs. Grass savannas, forest and wetlands offer a habitat for numerous bird species as well. The park borders on the Royal Manas National Park in Bhutan.

After the elk and the red deer, the sambar deer is the largest species of deer in the world. During the day it spends its time in the underbrush (below). The Kaziranga National Park is also home to one-horned rhinoceroses, water buffalo, and elephants. Right: An elephant safari in the park.

Kaziringa National Park

Kaziranga National Park is affected by the volatile tendencies of the Brahmaputra River. In July and August, the monsoon season, two-thirds of the park are flooded on a regular basis. Animals tend to then move to higher ground, sometimes even outside park territory.

Protection of the Indian rhinoceros has always been the highest priority for local animal conservationists. At the turn of the 20th century, the population had fallen so drastically that hunting permits were banned and in 1908, the area was declared a sanctuary. In 1950, it was designated a wildlife sanctuary and in 1974, it became a national park. Today, there are an estimated 1,500 rhinoceroses. There are also elephants, water buffaloes, different types of deer, gibbons, tigers and wild pigs. Rare birds such as the Bengal florican and the spot-billed pelican also make their home here.

The mountain railways of India – all UNESCO World Heritage Sites – are technical marvels with narrow-gauge tracks that twist spectacularly through the mountains. Two of the most famous lines are the Darjeeling Himalayan Railway (shown here) and the Nilgiri Mountain Railway.

THE TOY TRAIN TO DARJEELING

The nine-hour trip on this narrow-gauge railway from Siliguri in the Gangetic Plain to Darjeeling, the hill station and center of tea production, is an exciting experience. According to the timetable, the railway, also fondly called the "Toy Train", makes fourteen stops along its 88 km (54 miles) journey. Ghum, the station just before you reach Darjeeling, is located at an altitude of 2,175 m (7,136 ft) and is therefore one of the highest train stations in the world. The train winds its way upwards through countless curves and bends with imaginative names such as Agony Point and Sensation Corner. It is propelled by a venerable old steam locomotive housed in a signature blue carriage that is three times the width of the track on which it rolls. The railway line, which zigzags through the hills, was constructed between 1879 and 1881 by the British firm Gillander Arbuthnot & Co. to provide colonial administrators an escape from the unbearable heat of Calcutta. At the time, it was considered a marvel of engineering. Natural barriers and steep grades had to be overcome without resorting to rack or cable mechanisms. Its construction marked a significant advance for India economically speaking as well: It was the first train line in the country to be built solely with Indian capital.

The present official name of the Howrah Bridge is Rabindra Setu, in honor of the Bengali national poet Rabindranath Tagore. It is a legacy of colonial rule, as is the Victoria Memorial (top right). Below: One of the many vegetable markets.

Kolkata

Kolkata and its roughly fifteen million inhabitants are considered the poorhouse of India. Until 1911, it was the capital of British India and called Calcutta until 2001. Construction of the Victoria Memorial at the southern end of the Maidan, Kolkata's largest park, was financed by wealthy merchants in memory of Queen Victoria, who in 1877 became Empress of India. Another landmark is the Howrah Bridge over the Hugli River, a cantilevered structure hailed around the world as a technical wonder when it was completed in 1943. A sense of awakening is palpable in the intellectual capital of India. Technological parks are springing up on the outskirts, and high-tech companies here are growing at twice the rate of the national average. The country's economic boom is bringing new hope to the city with the world's largest tea exchange.

Far right: A satellite photo of the Sundarbans shows the mangrove forests as a dark green area, while the sediment-laden rivers appear a murky gray. Below: Chital deer are among the favorite prey of the Royal Bengal tiger (right).

Sundarbans National Park

Together with their common estuary, the Meghna, two vast rivers – the Ganges and the Brahmaputra – form the natural basis for the Sundarbans, the largest mangrove forest in the world. Over half of the area is within the Indian part of Bengal, while the rest lies in Bangladeshi territory. A transitional zone between salt- and freshwater, this rich ecological system of wetlands is a habitat for a huge variety of animals including otters, water snakes, turtles, water monitors, crocodiles, storks, cranes, cormorants, curlews, seagulls and terns, all of which are native to the area. The Sundarbans are also an important refuge for the critically endangered Bengal tiger. Smaller and with a more reddish coat than other Indian tigers, it hunts spotted deer and wild boar, but also often falls prey to man, despite its protected status.

Below: Large and elaborately carved sun wheels are the defining features of Konarak. Gods, musicians and even elephants are common motifs symbolic of the joy of life. Right: The temple complex is one of the most important Brahmanic shrines of ancient India.

Konarak

As far back as the Vedic Period, the sun god Surya formed a type of trinity with the fire god Agni and the thunder god Indra. As a giver of life, this deity has been worshipped by Hindus since time immemorial. The temple in Konarak was built in the 13th century and is a stone representation of the chariot in which the deity travels every day across the firmament. It follows that the twelve wheels on the walls at the temple's foundation symbolize the sun in two different ways: the circle of the wheel represents its shape, and the number of wheels stands for the twelve months the Earth needs to revolve around it. While the walls of the temple are decorated with figures, the surfaces of the tall base and the wheels, including their radiating spokes, are completely covered with intricate reliefs and stonework.

Inset: Looking down from Mount Anamudi, southern India's tallest mountain at 2,695 m (8,842 ft), you see tea plantations and the lush green grasslands of the Eravikulam National Park in Kerala.

This meticulously painted Kathakali dancer is made up as Prince Bima of the Indian Mahabharata epic. Bima is one of the designated pacca characters, "pacca" meaning "green" or "pure".

THE SUBTROPICAL SOUTH

Spared largely from the ravages of conquest by foreign invaders, southern India, homeland of the Dravidians, is widely seen as the heart of Hindu India. The subtropical landscapes of the southern Deccan Plateau stretch from the Malabar Coast in the west to the Coromandel Coast in the east. Sandy, palm-lined beaches and monsoon rainforests alternate with fertile river landscapes. In the south-west, the spectacular Nilgiri and Cardamom hills reach elevations of over 2,000 m (6,500 ft).

Below: The Shri Meenakshi Temple in Madurai is one of the largest in India. The temple of the dancing Shiva in Chidambaram is said to have been founded by Brahmins as far back as the year 500 AD. The present building is relatively new: It was built in 1000 AD.

Chidambaram, Madurai

No other Indian state has as many temples as Tamil Nadu. The enormous temple complexes here give you the impression that nowhere else do the gods reside so splendidly as in Tamil Nadu. In a cultural landscape that spans a thousand years, the capital Chennai (formerly Madras) is rather young. Fort St George, the first British fortress in India, dates from 1644, and is located not far from the sea. Inside the building, next to the Tamil Na-du government building, is St Mary's Church (1680), the oldest Anglican house of worship in India. The Chennai Egmore railway station and the Madras High Court are lovely examples of colonial architecture. South of the coastal road known as the "Marina", in the Mylapore District, is the St Thomas Cathedral with the tomb of St Thomas the Apostle. The fertile Cauvery Delta has made the land of the Tamils the rice bowl of India.

Below: The granite reliefs in the temple complex of Mahabalipuram, which illustrate the descent of the Ganges, are highlights of Indian sculpture. Impressive, realistically carved stone sculptures greet visitors at the Brihadishwara Temple in Thanjavur (right).

Mahabalipuram, Thanjavur

After Pallava King Narasimhavarman I, who reigned from 625 to 645, conquered some neighboring cities and thus became acquainted with the breathtaking architecture of the Chalukya rulers, he commissioned the beautification of his capital in Mahabalipuram. His efforts resulted in some of the most beautiful works of Dravidian architecture, whose forms from then on became synonymous with southern Indian styles. The five buildings here are rathas, not temples in the conventional sense, but rather monumental sculptures carved out of the living rock. While Ratha No.1 looks rather plain, Ratha No. 5, the Dharmaraja Ratha, became the prototype for numerous Dravidian temples. As such, the successor of Narasimhavarman built the Shore Temple of Mahabalipuram according to the Ratha pattern that his predecessor developed.

Below: His face painted red and black, wearing a magnificent headdress and a richly decorated costume, this Theyyam dancer is the embodiment of a local deity. It takes about two hours to put on the brilliant Kathakali mask (right) – and twice as long to remove it.

WHEN THE GODS DANCE

Classical Indian dance does not allow for improvisation. Every movement, every facial gesture, indeed, every muscle contraction has a meaning. When the gods dance, so goes the saying, the dancers become the intermediaries between heaven and earth. The dance is still considered sacred even if it is performed on a secular stage instead of in front of the temple shrine by the "devadasis", or dancers.

The oldest literary source for classical Indian dance is the Natya Shastra, a collection of texts written in Sanskrit in the 2nd century AD on the subjects of dance, theater, music and architecture. The texts are attributed to the sage Bharata, who is also referred to in the name of one of India's oldest solo dances, the Bharata Natyam ("Bharata's dance"), which is performed regularly as part of religious rituals, court ceremonials, weddings and other important social events. It comes from Tamil Nadu. The Kathakali, a dance-drama performed by men whose hand gestures and facial expressions are adapted from Kutiyyam, is the only surviving form of Sanskrit theatre and comes from the state of Kerala. Also from Kerala is the Mohiniyattam, a dance performed by women that depicts Vishnu's incarnation as the divine seductress Mohini (from the Sanskrit: "the enchantress").

Below: On the coast near Kochi, nets are drawn out of the water with the help of heavy stone counterweights. Right: Harvesting pepper on a spice plantation in Periyar National Park. Top right: A Keralan thali – an Indian meal – served on a banana leaf.

Kerala

The perennially green state of Kerala runs 520 km (325 miles) along the Malabar Coast where, in the year 52 AD, St Thomas the Apostle is said to have landed at Muziris. The Portuguese explorer Vasco da Gama landed in Calicut (now Kozhikode) in 1498, discovering the sea route from Europe to India. Cochin (Kochi) became the first European settlement in India around 1500. The port town is built on islands off the coast of its twin city, Ernakulam. The St Francis Church (1510) on the island of Mattancherry became the first Christian church in India. The Mattancherry Palace was built by the Portuguese in 1567, remodeled by the Dutch in 1663, and since then has been known as the "Dutch Palace". The neighboring Jewish quarter is a lively one and the street leading to the Paradesi Synagogue (1568) is lined with myriad shops including the traditional spice market.

Below: A taxi driver in Kolkata. "India demands a lot from its visitors. Most of the country has only two seasons instead of four: a hot season, and an even hotter one" – Khushwant Singh.

ATLAS

Over a billion people live in the seventh-largest (by area) and second-largest (by population) country on earth. Bordered in the north by the Himalayas, in the south-west by the Arabian Sea, in the south-east by the Bay of Bengal, and in the south by the Indian Ocean, it approximates the shape of a diamond on the map. Located between Africa and the Arabian peninsula to the west and Malaysia and the Indonesian archipelago to the east, India has a strategically central position.

In sharp contrast to the rural landscape left and right of the street, Jodhpur is the second-largest city in Rajasthan with 800,000 people. It is the south-eastern corner of the "great desert triangle".

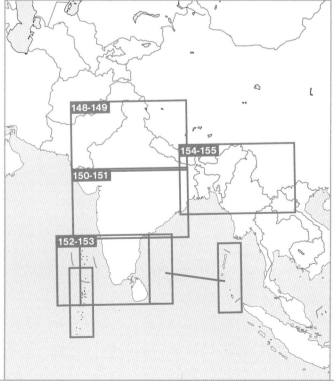

MAP LEGEND
1:4 500 000

══════ ::::::	Motorway (under construction)
══════════	Toll Motorway
═════ ::::::	Dual-lane Carriageway (under construction)
════ ::::::	Trunk Road (under construction)
═══ ::::::	Important Major Road (under construction)
──────	Major Road
──────	Minor Road
───────	Dirt Track
─·─·─·	Railway
──────	National and Nature Park
11	Motorway Number
40	Other Road Number
═══▯═══	Junction
⊗	Motorway Restaurant and Motel
✈	Major Airport
✈	Airport
✈	Airfield
⛴	Car Ferry

LEGEND

The maps on the following pages show India on a scale of 1:450,000. The geographical details have been supplemented by a great deal of interesting information for travelers including public transportation networks and smart pictograms indicating the locations and types of sights and holiday destinations. The names of cities of interest for travelers are also highlighted in yellow along with monuments that are UNESCO World Heritage Sites.

ICONS

Renowned routes
- 🚗 Car Route
- 🚆 Railway
- 🚢 Ship Route

Natural landscapes and monuments
- ■ UNESCO World Natural Heritage Site
- 🏔 Mountainous Landscape
- Glacier
- Volcano, extinct
- Rocky Landscape
- Gorge/Canyon
- Cave
- River Landscape
- Waterfall/Rapids
- Lakeland Area
- Dune Landscape
- Oasis

- Nature Park
- National Park (fauna)
- National Park (flora)
- National Park (culture)
- National Park (landscape)
- Coastal Landscape
- Island
- Beach
- Coral Reef
- Protected Underwater Area
- Fossil Finds
- Wildlife Sanctuary
- Sea Turtle Sanctuary/Observation Area

Cultural monuments and events
- ☐ UNESCO World Cultural Heritage Site
- ☐ Remarkable City
- Prehistory and Early History

- Ancient Orient
- Old India
- Old China
- Islamic Cultural Site
- Jewish Cultural Site
- Buddhism
- Hinduism
- Christian Cultural Site
- Jainism
- Sikhs
- Other Religions
- Cultural Landscape
- Castle/Fortress/Fortifications
- Palace/Chateau
- Mirror and Radio Telescope
- Historic Old Town
- Museum
- Monument
- Tomb
- Market

- Theater of War/Battle Field
- Prominent Bridge

Sport and leisure destinations
- Ski Area
- Sailing
- Canoeing/Rafting
- Surfing
- Diving
- Mineral Baths/Hot Springs
- Swimming
- Leisure Park
- Hill Resort
- Seaport

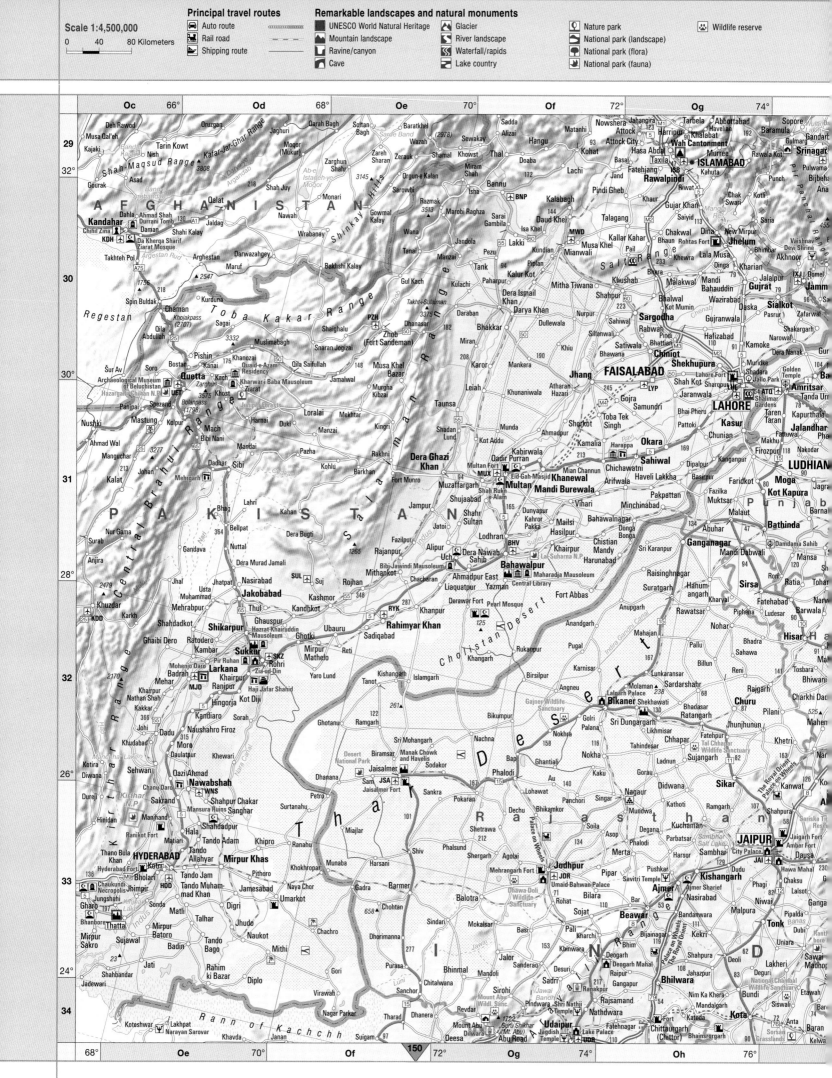

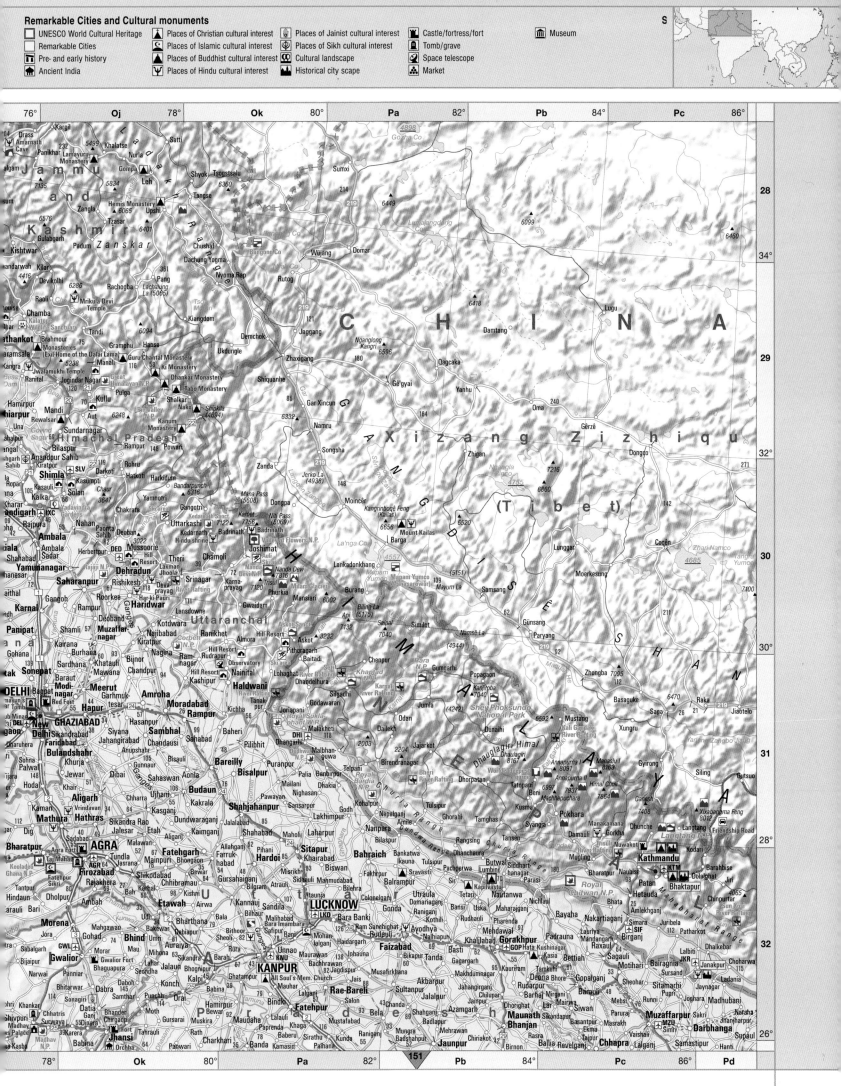

Remarkable Cities and Cultural monuments

- ☐ UNESCO World Cultural Heritage
- ☐ Remarkable Cities
- ⫟ Pre- and early history
- 🏛 Ancient India
- ☪ Places of Christian cultural interest
- ☪ Places of Islamic cultural interest
- ⚑ Places of Buddhist cultural interest
- Ψ Places of Hindu cultural interest
- ⛩ Places of Jainist cultural interest
- ☬ Places of Sikh cultural interest
- ⊕ Cultural landscape
- ◤ Historical city scape
- ⛫ Castle/fortress/fort
- ⛨ Tomb/grave
- ⊡ Space telescope
- ⊞ Market
- 🏛 Museum

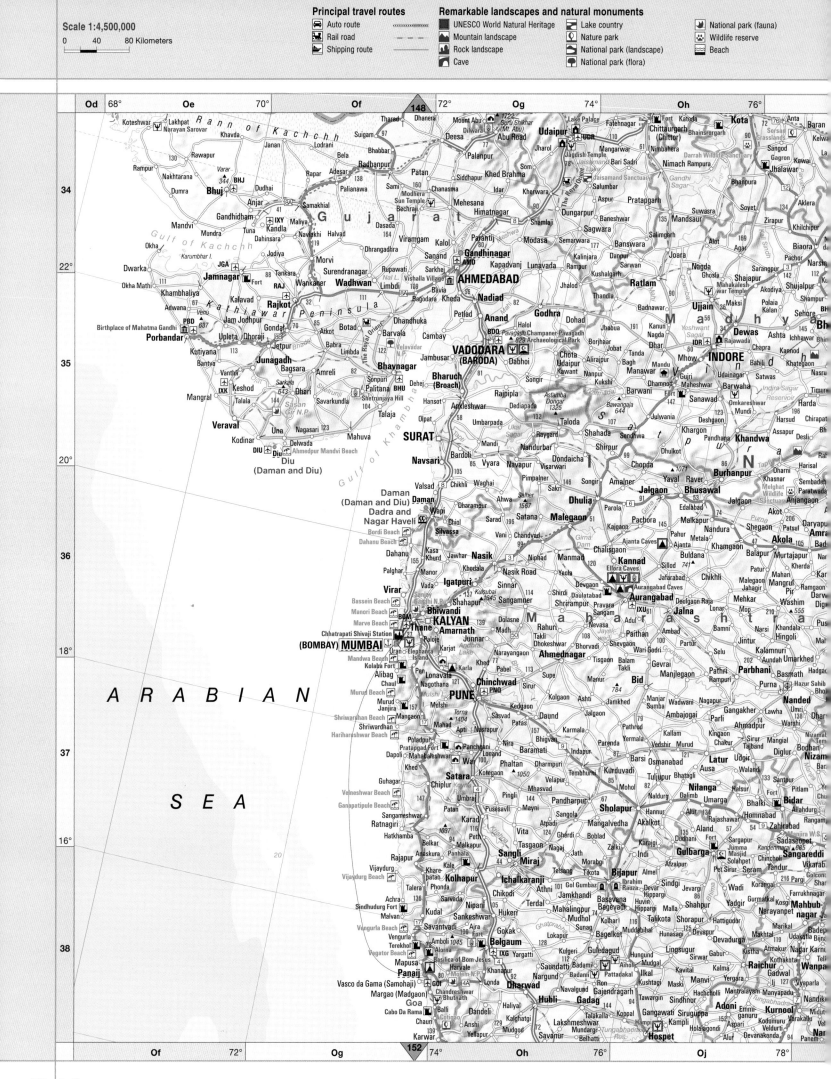

Scale 1:4,500,000

0   40   80 Kilometers

Principal travel routes

🚗 Auto route
🚂 Rail road
🚢 Shipping route

Remarkable landscapes and natural monuments

🏞 UNESCO World Natural Heritage
⛰ Mountain landscape
🪨 Rock landscape
🕳 Cave

🌊 Lake country
🌿 Nature park
🏕 National park (landscape)
🌸 National park (flora)

🦌 National park (fauna)
🦓 Wildlife reserve
🏖 Beach

ARABIAN

SEA

Gujarat

Maharashtra

Madhya

Goa

Principal travel routes

- ⊞ Auto route ┈┈┈┈
- ⊞ Rail road ┉ ┉ ┉
- ⊞ Shipping route ───

Remarkable landscapes and natural monuments

- ⬛ UNESCO World Natural Heritage
- ⬛ Mountain landscape
- ⬛ River landscape
- ⬛ Waterfall/rapids
- ⬛ Nature park
- ⬛ National park (landscape)
- ⬛ National park (flora)
- ⬛ National park (fauna)
- ⬛ Wildlife reserve
- ⬛ Turtle conservation area
- ⬛ Coastal landscape
- ⬛ Coral reef
- ⬛ Island
- ⬛ Underwater reserve

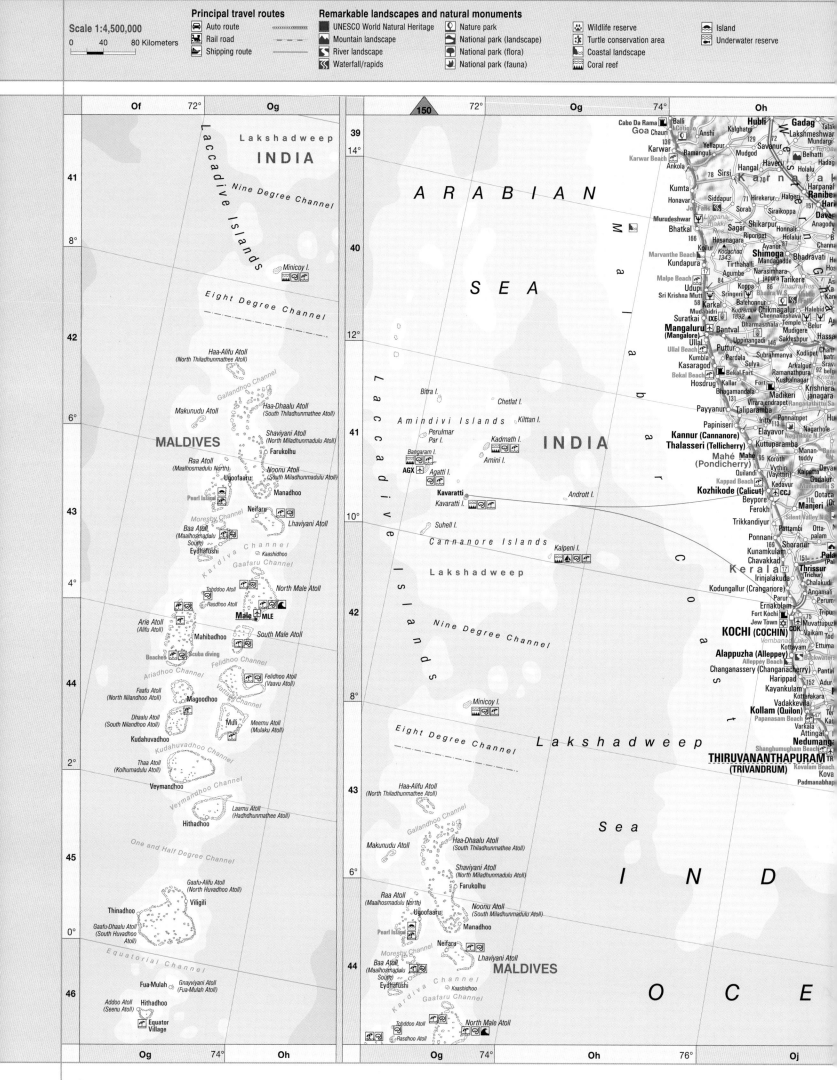

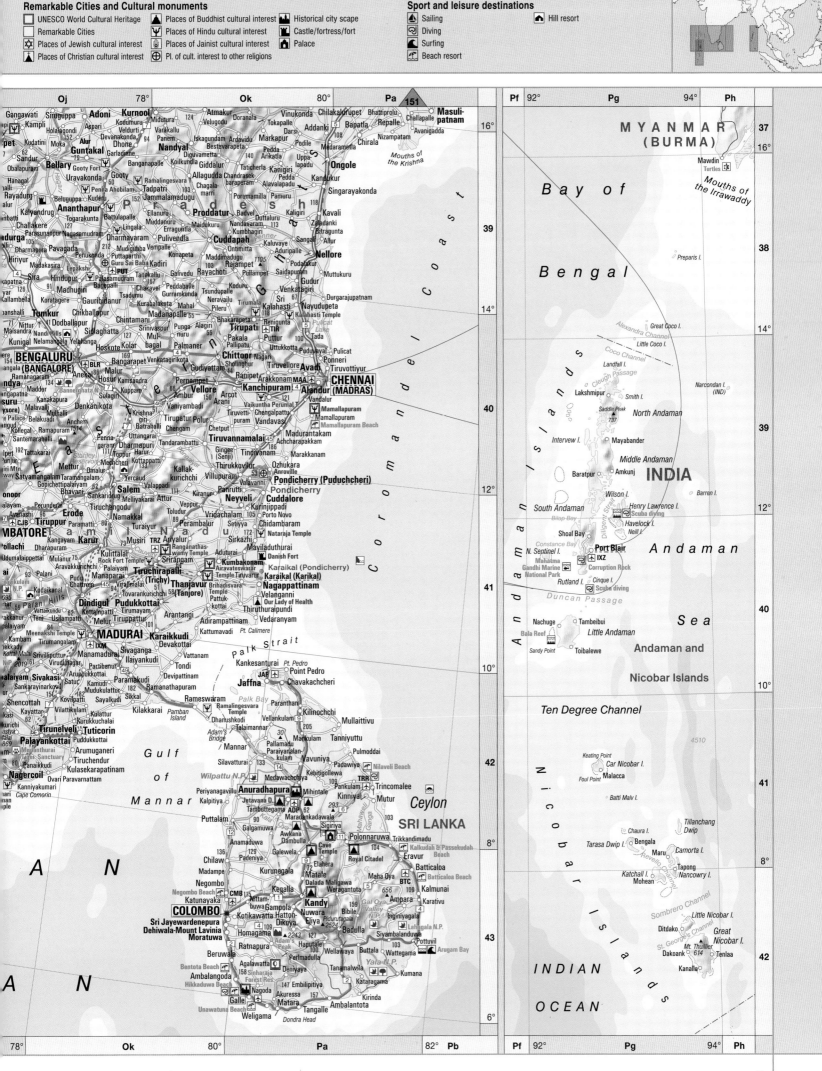

Remarkable Cities and Cultural monuments

☐ UNESCO World Cultural Heritage
☐ Remarkable Cities
✡ Places of Jewish cultural interest
▲ Places of Christian cultural interest
⛩ Places of Buddhist cultural interest
♁ Places of Hindu cultural interest
⚏ Places of Jainist cultural interest
⊕ Pl. of cult. interest to other religions
⛫ Historical city scape
⛉ Castle/fortress/fort
⛪ Palace

Sport and leisure destinations

⛵ Sailing
⚓ Diving
🏄 Surfing
🏖 Beach resort

⌂ Hill resort

Oj · 78° · Ok · 80° · Pa · 151

Pf · 92° · Pg · 94° · Ph

MYANMAR (BURMA)

37 · 16°

Mawdin
Turtles

Gangawati · Siruppa · **Adoni** · **Kurnool** · Atmakur · Doranala · Vinukonda · Chilakalurupet · Bhattiprolu · Challapalle · **Masuli-patnam**
Kampli · Holalagondi · Aspari · Midutura · 124 · Velugodu · Darsi · Addanki · Bapatla · Repalle · Avanigadda
Kudatini · Moka · Kodumuru · Veldurti · Varakallu · Iskagunta · Markapur · Podile · Nizampatam

Bay of Bengal

Preparis I.

Mouths of the Krishna

Mouths of the Irrawaddy

India · 153

Remarkable Cities and Cultural monuments

- ☐ UNESCO World Cultural Heritage
- ☐ Remarkable Cities
- 🌙 Ancient China
- ☪ Places of Islamic cultural interest
- ▲ Places of Buddhist cultural interest
- ⚏ Places of Hindu cultural interest
- ⚏ Places of Jainist cultural interest
- ⚏ Pl. of cult. interest to indig. peoples
- ∞ Cultural landscape
- 🏰 Historical city scape
- 🏰 Castle/fortress/fort
- 🏛 Palace

Sport and leisure destinations

- 🚣 Canoeing/rafting
- ⛱ Beach resort
- ♨ Mineral/thermal spa
- 🏔 Hill resort
- 🚀 Space mission launch site
- 🌉 Remarkable bridge
- ✗ Theater of war/battlefield
- 🏛 Museum

The index listings refer to the section of the picture and the maps. After the keyword is a pictogram that refers to the point of interest according to the map entry (see pg. 147). The page number and keyword entry for the map section are in bold. After that is the page number for the picture and finally there are Internet addresses where you can quickly find current information about the locations and sights mentioned in this volume. Most of the entries on the image pages are also in the maps, which give you additional helpful travel information.

"If there is one place where all of your dreams – after all, people have been dreaming since day one – have found a home, then it is India" – Romain Rolland. Top, from left: A snow leopard; two women in Ladakh; in the temple district of Amritsar; a Sadhu in Amber.

Mumbai ⊙ ☒	150	Og36		www.mcgm.gov.in
			96, 108, 110	
Murud Beach ☒	150	Og36		www.konkandarshan.com/tourist/r_murud.htm
Murudeshwar ☒	152	Oh39		www.karnataka.com/tourism/murdeshwar
Mysore = Mysuru ⊙	153	Oj40		www.mysore.org.uk
Mysore Palace ⬛	153	Oj40		www.mysore.org.uk/royal-buildings/mysore-palace.html
Mysuru ⊙	153	Oj40		http://mysore.nic.in
Nagarhole National Park ☒	152	Oh41		www.india-wildlife-tours.com/wildlife-packages
Nagarjunakonda ▲	151	Ok37		www.buddhist-pilgrimage.com/nagarjuna-konda.html
Nagarjunasagar-Srisailam Sanctuary ☒	151	Ok37		www.indiantigers.com/nagarjunsagar-national-park.html
Nagaur ⊙ ▲	148	Og32		http://nagaur.nic.in
Nako ▲	149	Ok30		http://himachaltourism.nic.in/kinn.htm
Namdhapa National Park ☒	155	Pj32		www.indiantigers.com/namdapha-tigers-park.html
Nameri National Park ☒	154	Pg32		http://projecttiger.nic.in/nameri.htm
Nanda Devi ▲	149	Pa30	10	www.summitpost.org/mountain/rock
Nanda Devi National Park ■ ☒	149	Ok30		http://whc.unesco.org/en/list/335
Nandankanan Biological Park ⊙	151	Pc35		www.geocities.com/nandankananorissa
Nandi Hills ☒	153	Oj40		http://horticulture.kar.nic.in/nandi.htm
Narasimha Temple (Hampi)			119	
Narayan Sarovar ☒	150	Oe34		www.gujaratguideonline.com/Kutch-Places.html
Nasik ⊙	150	Og36	62	www.nashik.nic.in
Nataraja Temple ☒	153	Ok41		www.tamilnadutourism.org/places/citiestowns
National Chambal Wildlife Sanctuary ☒	148	Oj33		http://rajforest.nic.in/national_chambal.htm
National Park Eravikulam = Eravikulam National Park			134	
National Park Kaziranga = Kaziranga National Park			124	
National Park Keoladeo = Keoladeo Ghana National Park			88	
National Park Periyar = Periyar National Park			142	
National Park Sundarbans = Sundarbans National Park			130	
Navegaon National Park ☒	151	Pa35		www.indiawildliferesorts.com/national-parks
Nawalgar			74	
New Delhi ●			32	
New Delhi ●	149	Oh31		www.delhigate.com/main.htm
Nilgiri Mtn. Railway □ ☒	153	Oj41		http://whc.unesco.org/en/list/944
Nizamabad Temple ☒	150	Ok36		www.indiatourism.com/andhra-pradesh-pilgrim-centres
Nrusinghanath Temple ☒	151	Pc35		http://orissadiary.com/orissa_tourism/temple
Observatory (Jaipur)			81	
Omkareshwar ☒	150	Oj34		www.mptourism.com/dest/omkareshwar.html
Orchha ⬛	151	Ok33		www.mptourism.com/dest/orchha.html
Our Lady of Health (Velanganni) ▲	153	Ok41		www.annaivailankanni.org
Pachmarhi Hill Resort ☒	151	Ok34		www.hillresortsinindia.com/pachmarhi.html
Padmanabhapuram ⬛	153	Oj42		www.trivandrumonline.com/travelinformation
Palace on Wheels ☒	148	Oh32		www.palaceonwheels.net
Palace of the Winds (Jaipur) = Hawa Mahal			80	
Palamau National Park ☒	151	Pc34		www.tourism-of-india.com/palamau.html
Panchgani Hill Resort ☒	150	Og37		www.incredibleindiatravel.com/hill-resorts-in-india
Panhala ☒	150	Oh37		http://panhala.org
Panna National Park ☒	151	Pa33		www.wildlife-tour-india.com/wildlife-in-india
Papanasam Beach ☒	152	Oj42		www.varkkala.com/pages/2attractions.htm
Patna Sahib ☒	151	Pc33		www.sikhtourism.com/patna-sahib.htm
Pattadakal □ ☒	150	Oh38	114	http://whc.unesco.org/en/list/239
Pawapuri ☒	151	Pc33		http://bstdc.bih.nic.in/Pawapuri.htm
Pench National Park ☒ ☒	151	Ok35		www.pench.net
Penna Ahobilam ☒	153	Oj39		www.anantapur.com/travel/penna.html
Periyar National Park ☒	153	Oj42		www.india-wildlife-tours.com/wildlife-packages
Pin Valley National Park ☒	149	Ok30		http://hplahaulspiti.gov.in/pinpark.htm
Pithoragarh Hill Resort ☒	149	Pa31		www.uttaranchaltourism.in/mussoorie.html
Pithoragarh Ski area ☒	149	Pa31		www.visit-himalaya.com/adventure-in-himalayas
Pratapgad Fort ☒	150	Og37		www.maharashtratourism.net/forts/pratapgad-fort.html
Presidential Palace (Delhi)			38	
Puri ⊙ ☒	151	Pc36		http://puri.nic.in
Puri Beach ☒	151	Pc36		www.orissatourism.org/orissa-beaches/puri-beach.html
Pushkar ☒	148	Oh32	82	www.rajasthantourism.gov.in/new/site/Destinations
Pushkar-See			83	
Qutb-Komplex (Delhi)			44	
Qutb Minar (Delhi) = Qutub Minar			46	
Qutub Minar □ ☒	149	Oj31		http://whc.unesco.org/en/list/233
Rajaji National Park ☒	149	Oj30		www.rajajinationalpark.in
Rajasthan ⊙	148	Og32	70, 72, 76, 81, 87	
Rajawada (Indore) ⬛	150	Oh34		www.mptourism.com/dest/ind_ms.html
Ramalingesvara Temple ☒	153	Ok33		www.hindubooks.org/temples/andhrapradesh/tadpatri
Ramalingesvara Temple ☒	153	Ok42		www.rameswaramtemple.org

Ramanathaswamy Temple (Rameswaram) ☒	153	Ok42		www.tourism-southindia.com/south-india-temples
Rameswaram ⊙	153	Ok42		www.rameswaram.co.in
Ranakpur ☒	148	Og33	100, 146	www.rajasthantourism.gov.in/new/site/Destinations
Ranganathaswamy Temple □ ☒	153	Oj41		www.srirangam.org
Ranganathittu Sanctuary ⊙	152	Oj40		www.mysore.org.uk
Ranthambore National Park ☒	148	Oj32		www.ranthamborenationalpark.com
Ratnagiri ▲	154	Pd35		http://ratnagiri.nic.in
Rayadurg ⊙ ☒	153	Oj39		www.india9.com/i9show/Rayadurg-67891.htm
Red Fort (Delhi) □ ☒	149	Oj31	40	http://asi.nic.in/asi_monu_tktd_delhi_redfort.asp
Red Fort (Agra) = Agra Fort			50	
Rewalsar ☒	149	Oj30		http://hptdc.nic.in/cir0202.htm
River Rafting (Devaprayag) ☒	149	Ok30		www.eastmanvoyages.com/north.html
River Rafting (Tanakpur) ☒	149	Pa31		www.journeymart.com
Rock Fort Temple (Trichy) ☒	153	Ok41		www.bharatonline.com/tamilnadu/travel/tiruchirapalli
Rohtas ☒	151	Pb33		www.rohtasfort.com
Rutland Island ☒	153	Pg40		http://tourism.andaman.nic.in/diving.htm
Sanchi □ ▲	151	Oj34	102	http://whc.unesco.org/en/list/524
Sanchi ⊙	151	Oj34	102	www.mptourism.com/dest/sanchi.html
Sangam (Allahabad) ☒	151	Pa33		up-tourism.com/destination/allahabad
Sanjay Gandhi National Park ☒	150	Og36		www.borivlinationalpark.com
Sariska Tiger Reserve ☒	148	Oj32		www.rajasthantourism.gov.in/attractions
Sarnath ☒	151	Pb33		www.buddhanet.net/e-learning/buddhistworld
Sasan Gir National Park ☒	150	Of35		http://members.rediff.com/sumit_sen/gir.htm
Satpura Range ☒	150	Oh35		http://members.rediff.com/sumit_sen/satpura.htm
Savitri Temple ☒	148	Oh32		www.wondersofrajasthan.com
Sé Cathedral (Goa)			117	www.indiatourism.com/goa-churches
Shah-Hamadan Mosque (Srinagar)			14	http://srinagar.nic.in/districtprofile
Shanghumugham Beach ☒	152	Oj42		www.tourismofkerala.com/beaches/otherbeaches.html
Shekhawati ⊙ ☒	148	Og31	74	www.apanidhani.com/shekha
Shetrunjaya Hill ☒	150	Of35		www.ahmedabadcity.com
Shree Meenakshi Sundareswarwar Temple = Meenakshi Temple ☒	153	Oj42		www.maduraimeenakshi.org
Shri-Meenakshi Temple (Madurai) = Meenakshi Temple			136	www.maduraimeenakshi.org
Shri Nathji Temple ☒	148	Og33		www.udaipur.indiainformation.com
Shriwardhan Beach ☒	150	Og36		http://beachesinindia.com/shriwardhnbeach.htm
Sikkim ⊙	154	Pe32	31	
Silent Valley National Park ☒ ☒	153	Oj41		www.indiawildliferesorts.com/national-parks
Similipal National Park ☒	154	Pd35		http://projecttiger.nic.in/similipal.htm
Sindhudurg Fort ☒	150	Og37		www.maharashtratourism.gov.in
Sivaram Wildlife Sanctuary ☒	151	Ok36		www.bharatonline.com/andhra-pradesh/travel/adilabad
Sonagiri ☒	149	Ok33		http://datia.nic.in/sonagiri.htm
Sonai-Rupa National Park ☒	154	Pg32		
Sorsan Grasslands ⊙	150	Oj33		www.indiasite.com/rajasthan/kota/darrah.html
Sravanabelgola ☒	152	Oj40	100	www.grant.org/plewins/india2000/Kerala/Statue.html
Sravasti ▲	149	Pb32		www.sravastiabbey.org
Sri Krishna Mutt (Udupi) ☒	152	Oh40		www.dvaita.org/madhva/udupi/krishna_mutt.html
Srinagar ⊙	148	Oh28	14	http://srinagar.nic.in
Sringeri ☒	152	Oh40		www.sringeri.net
Sundarbans National Park ■ ☒ ☒	154	Pe34		http://whc.unesco.org/en/list/452
Sun Temple (Konark) □ ☒	154	Pd36		http://konark.nic.in
Tabo Monastery ▲	149	Ok29		www.aarogya.com/tabo/monastery.html
Tadoba-Andhari National Park ☒	151	Ok35		http://projecttiger.nic.in/tadoba.htm
Taj Mahal (Agra) □ ⬛	149	Oj32		
			6, 52, 54	www.up-tourism.com/destination/agra/agra.htm
Tal Chhapar Wildlife Sanctuary ☒	148	Oh32		www.indiatraveldestinations.com
Terekhol ☒	150	Og38		www.bharatonline.com/goa/goa-travel/pernem
Thanjavur ⊙	153	Ok41	138	
Thar Desert ☒	148	Of32	71, 76	www.worldwildlife.org
The Royal Orient ☒	148	Oh32		www.royalorienttrain.com
Tirumala ☒	153	Ok40		www.tirumala.org
Udaigiri ▲	154	Pd35		www.buddhist-temples.com/orissa/udaigiri.html
Udaipur ⊙	150	Og33	92	www.udaipurtourism.com
Udayagiri Caves ☒	151	Oj34		www.mptourism.com/dest/sanchi_exc.html
Udayagiri Caves ☒	151	Pc35		www.orissatourism.org/udayagiri-khandagiri-caves.html
Udaypur ☒	151	Ok34		http://vidisha.nic.in/Tourism_3.htm
Udhagamandalam = Ootacamund/Ooty ⊙	152	Oj41		www.ooty.com
Ujjain ⊙	150	Oh34	62	
Ullal Beach ☒	152	Oh40		www.ullaltown.gov.in/tourism.html
Umaid-Bahwan Palace ⬛	148	Og32	91	www.maharajodhpur.com/ubp/ubp_main.htm
Uttarkashi ski area ☒	149	Ok30		http://uttarkashi.nic.in/Dept/tourism/place_interest.htm
Uttar Pradesh State Astronomical Observatory ☒	149	Ok31		http://asi.nic.in/asi_monu_tktd_up_mansingh.asp
Vagator Beach ☒	150	Og38		www.indianbeachresorts.com/goa-beach-tour
Vaikuntha Perumal Temple ☒	153	Ok40		http://kanchi.nic.in/vaikunda.htm
Vaishnav Devi Shrine ☒	148	Oh29		www.vaishnavdevi.com
Valley of Flowers National Park ☒	149	Ok30	10	
Valley of Spiti			22	

Top, from left: The Taj Mahal; audience hall in the City Palace of Jaipur; the Thar Desert; a Teyyam dancer; two "sky-clad" worshippers at the feet of Gommateshavara in Sravana; red henna designs on the hands of a woman in Srinagar. Below: Jaisalmer.

Picture Credits

Abbreviations:

A	Alamy
C	Corbis
CE	Clemens Emmler
G	Getty
L	Laif
MM	Michael Martin
P	Premium

t = top, b = bottom, c = center, l = left,
r = right

Numbering from top left to bottom right

1 G/Ann&Steve Toon, 2/3 A/Imagebroker, 4/5 L/hemis, 6/7 P, 8 OK, 8/9 OK, 10.1 Biosphoto/BIOS, 10.2 Wildlife, 10.3 Biosphoto/NouN, 10/11 A/Dinodia Images, 12 Bilderberg/Dinodia, 12/13 L/hemis, 14 L/hemis, 14/15 L/hemis, 15.1 KM, 15.2 L/Hilger, 15.3 KM, 16.1 L/Gamma/Lafarge Daniel, 16.2 L/Aurora, 16.3 L/Hilger, 16.4 L/TCS, 16/17 L/hemis, 18.1 OK, 18.2 L/hemis, 18.3 L/Glogowski, 18/19 G/James Gritz, 20.1 L/hemis, 20.2 L/hemis, 20.3 L/TCS, 20/21 L/hemis, 22.1 Udo Bernhart, 22.2 Vario Images, 22.3 Vario Images, 22/23 OK, 24.1 C/Janez Skok, 24.2 A/Eagle Visions Photography/Craig Lovell, 24.3 A/Fiona Jeffrey, 24/25 G/National Geographic/Bruce Dale, 26.1 OK, 26.2 OK, 26.3 L/hemis, 26/27 G/The Image Bank/Mark Oatney, 28 C/epa/Raminder Pal Singh, 28/29 EyeUbiquitous/Hutchinson, 30 L/Le Figaro Magazine, 30/31 KM, 32 KM, 32/33 A/David Noton Photography, 34 G/AFP, 34/35 G/AFP/Narinder Nanu, 36 L/hemis, 36/37 OK, 38.1 L/Modrow, 38.2 G/Photographer's Choice/Cesat Lucas Abreu, 38.3 A/Rachael Bowes, 38.4 G/Lonely Planet Images/Paul Beinssen, 38.5 G/Lonely Planet Images/Richard I'Anson, 39.1 L/Modrow, 39.2 G/Win Initiative, 39.3 OK, 39.4 G/Lonely Planet Images/Richard I'Anson, 39.5 G/ Photographer's Choice/Cesat Lucas Abreu, 40.1 C/Lindsay Hebberd, 40.2 A/Susan Schulman, 40.3 A/Asia/Roger Cracknell 14, 42.1 A/Realimage, 42.2 A1PIX/JTB, 42/43 L/hemis, 44 C/Justin Guariglia, 44/45 C/Macduff Everton, 46 C, 46/47 C/Macduff Everton, 47 C/Macduff Everton, 48.1 G/AFP/Prakash Singh, 48.2 A/ArkReligion. com, 48/49 A/Neil Grant, 49 G/Renaud Visage, 50 A/Jake Norton, 50/51 C/Blaine Harrington III, 51 A/Steve Allen, 52.1 Premium/Bronsteen/Pan. Images, 52.2 KM, 52/53 L/hemis, 54 akg-images/Jean-Louis Nou, 54/55 akg-images/Jean-Louis Nou, 55.1 akg-images, 55.2 akg-images/Jean-Louis Nou, 55.3 akg-images/ Jean-Louis Nou, 55.4 akg-images/Jean-Louis Nou, 55.5 akg-images/Jean-Louis Nou, 55.6 Arco Images/H. Straesser, 55.7 akg-images/Jean-Louis Nou, 55.8 akg-images/Jean-Louis Nou, 55.9 akg-images/Jean-Louis Nou, 56 OK, 56/57 L/Lewis, 58.1 A/infocusphotos. com, 58.2 A/Grant Rooney, 58/59 L/Lewis, 60.1 C/Blaine Harrington III, 60.2 C/Angelo Hornak, 60.3 C/Angelo Hornak, 60.4 C/Travel Ink/Abbie Enock, 60/61 A/PhotosIndia. com LLC, 62 G/AFP/Manan Vatsyayana, 62/63 C/Reuters, 63.1 C/Sygma/Frédréric Soltan, 63.2 C/Reuters, 63.3 C/Kazuyoshi Nomachi, 64.1 G/Panoramic Images, 64.2 G, 64/65 L/hemis, 66.1 Blickwinkel/J. Royan, 66.2 Dieter Glogowski, 66.3 Premium/Buss, 66.4 FAN/Potschka, 66.5 Dieter Glogowski, 67.1 Dieter Glogowski, 67.2 Dieter Glogowski, 67.3 Dieter Glogowski, 67.4 Dieter Glogowski, 68.1 A/Robert Preston, 68.2 L/hemis, 68/69 A/Maciej Wojtkowiak, 70 L/Modrow, 70/71 Schapowalow/Robert Harding, 72.1 L/hemis, 72.2 L/hemis, 72.3 L/Reporters, 72/73 L/hemis, 73.1 A/John Arnold Images Ltd., 73.2 L/Gartung, 73.3 C/Brian A. Vikander, 73.4 C/Brian A. Vikander, 73.5 A/Tim Cuff, 74 C/Eye Ubiquitous/David Cumming, 74/75 L/hemis, 75 L/hemis, 76.1 G/Panoramic Images, 76.2 C/Bob Krist, 76.3 L/hemis, 76/77 G/Glen Allison, 78.1 G/Glowimages, 78.2 G/Panoramic Images, 78/79 A/Images Etc Ltd, 80.1 Fnoxx/Hettrich, 80.2 A/Martin Harvey, 80.3 L/hemis, 80.4 A/TNT Magazine, 80/81 C/Dve Bartruff, 82 ifa-Bilderteam/John Arnold Images, 82/83 A/Yadid Levy, 84.1 G/The Image Bank/Andrea Pistolesi, 84.2 A/Tibor Bognar, 84/85 A/Simon Reddy, 86 L/hemis, 86/87 L/Modrow, 88 Arco Images/Jorens-Belde 88/89 Okapia, 89.1 Okapia, 89.2 Blickwinkel/M. Woike, 89.3 Okapia, 90 G/Stone/Allison, 90/91 L/Harscher, 91.1 A/Iconotek, 91.2 L/hemis, 91.3 L/hemis, 92.1 G/Ernst Haas, 92.2 G/Eric Meola, 92.3 A/Tibor Bognar, 92.4 L/hemis, 92.5 L/hemis, 92/93 L/hemis, 93.1 C/Michael Freeman, 94.1 G, 94.2 G, 94.3 G, 94/95 L/hemis, 95 L/Modrow, 96 A/John Arnold Images Ltd., 96/97 A/Dinodia Images, 98.1 A/J. Marshall – Tribaleye, 98.2 L/hemis, 98.3 Mediacolors/Flueeler, 98/99 L/hemis, 99.1 OK, 99.2 C/Lindsay Hebberd, 99.3 L/hemis, 99.4 L/hemis, 99.5 OK, 100.1 A/Blaine Harrington III, 100.2 C/Jim Zuckerman, 100.3 A/Blaine Harrington III, 100/101 C/Christophe Boisvieux, 102 C/Atlantide Phototravel, 102/103 C/Atlantide Phototravel, 104.1 L/hemis, 104.2 L/On Asia/Graham Harrison, 104.3 L/On Asia/ Graham Harrison, 104.4 bridgemanart. com, 104/105 L/Kirchner, 106.1 A/David R. Frazier Photolibrary Inc., 106.2 C/Lindsay Hebbred, 106/107 L/Kirchner, 108 L/Heuer, 108/109 L/Roemers, 109 agenda/Joerg Boethling, 110-111 (17) agenda/Joerg Boethling, 112.1 A/David Pearson, 112.2 A/David Pearson, 112.3 C/Christophe Boisvieux, 112/113 C/Atlantide Phototravel, 114 L/hemis, 114/115 KM, 116.1 A/Robert Preston, 116.2 A/Robert Preston, 116.3 L/Huber, 116.4 L/Huber, 116/117 A/Peter Adams Photography, 118.1 L/Huber, 118.2 Natasa Trifunovic, 118.3 L/hemis, 118/119 Mediacolors/ Flueeler, 119 KM, 120 OK, 120/121 biosphoto/Allofs Theo, 122 Okapia, 122/123 Okapia, 123 Wildlife, 124 C/Lindsay Hebberd, 124/125 A/Nature Picture Library, 125.1 Okapia, 125.2 A/Kevin Schafer, 125.3 A/Nature Picture Library, 126.1 L/Le Figaro Magazine, 126.2 L/Westrich, 126.3 A/ Sherab, 126/127 A/maciej Wojtkowiak, 127 C/Macduff Everton, 128.1 G/AFP, 128.2 A/Indiapicture, 128/129 L/hemis, 130.1 Wildlife, 130.2 Wildlife, 130.3 Wildlife, 130/131 Mustafiz Mamun/ Majority World, 131 Geospace, 132.1 A/Neil Mc Allister, 132.2 L/hemis, 132.3 Bildagentur-online, 132.4 Bildarchiv Monheim/Rainer Kiedrowski, 132/133 C/Christophe Boisvieux, 134 OK, 134/135 L/Huber, 136.1 L/Huber, 136.2 L/Huber, 136/137 L/hemis, 137 L/Olivier Foellmi, 138.1 A/Eddie Gerald, 138.2 L/Le Figaro Magazine, 138.3 A/Deepak Dogra, 138/139 A/travelib india, 140.1 Premium/ Stock Images/S. Held, 140.2 L/Huber, 140.3 L/Huber, 140/141 Paysan, 142.1 L/Huber, 142.2 OK, 142/143 A/David Pearson, 144/145 L/hemis, 146/147 C/Freeman

This edition is published on behalf of APA Publications GmbH & Co. Verlag KG, Singapore Branch, Singapore by Verlag Wolfgang Kunth GmbH & Co KG, Munich, Germany

Distribution of this edition:

**GeoCenter International Ltd
Meridian House, Churchill Way West
Basingstoke, Hampshire RG21 6YR
Great Britain
Tel.: (44) 1256 817 987
Fax: (44) 1256 817 988
sales@geocenter.co.uk
www.insightguides.com**

ISBN 978-981-282-004-4

Original edition:
© 2008 Verlag Wolfgang Kunth GmbH & Co. KG, Munich
Königinstr. 11
80539 Munich
Ph: +49.89.45 80 20-0
Fax: +49.89.45 80 20-21
www.kunth-verlag.de

English edition:
Copyright © 2008 Verlag Wolfgang Kunth GmbH & Co. KG
© Cartography: GeoGraphic Publishers GmbH & Co. KG

All rights reserved. Reproduction, storage in data-processing facilities, reproduction by electronic, photomechanical and similar means only with the express permission of the copyright holder.

Text: Claudia Penner, Robert Fischer
Translation: Jose Medina
Editor: Kevin White for bookwise Medienproduktion GmbH, Munich
Production: bookwise Medienproduktion GmbH, Munich

Printed in Slovakia

The information and facts presented in this book have been extensively researched and edited for accuracy. The publishers, authors, and editors, cannot, however, guarantee that all of the information in the book is entirely accurate or up to date at the time of publication. The publishers are grateful for any suggestions or corrections that would improve the content of this book.